# Cabin Number 5

Coastal British Columbia is Supernatural!

*Wayne J. ...*

Lulu Edition

1st Edition printed 2012: ISBN 978-0-9867319-0-7

Note for Librarians: a catalog record for this book that includes Dewey Decimal Classification and U.S. Library of Congress numbers is available from the Library and Archives of Canada. The complete catalog record can be obtained from their online database at:

www.collectionscanada.ca/amicus/index-e.html

ISBN 978-0-9867319-0-7

**Printed in the United States by Lulu.com**

# Powell River Books

Powell RIver, BC

Book sales online at:
www.powellriverbooks.com
phone: 604-483-1704
email: wlutz@mtsac.edu

10 9 8 7 6 5 4 3 2 1

# Cabin Number 5
## Coastal British Columbia Stories

*Wayne J. Lutz*

*2012*
*Powell River Books*

To John...

An aquatic engineer
who builds skookum float cabins

The stories are true, and the characters are real.
All of the mistakes rest solely with the author.

# Other Books by Wayne J. Lutz

## *Costal British Columbia Stories*
*Up the Lake*
*Up the Main*
*Up the Winter Trail*
*Up the Strait*
*Up the Airway*
*Farther Up the Lake*
*Farther Up the Main*
*Farther Up the Strait*

## *Science Fiction Titles*
*Echo of a Distant Planet*
*Inbound to Earth*

---

**Front Cover Photo:**
Cabin Number 5, Powell Lake BC

**Back Cover Photos:**
**Top:** Construction of Cedar Float at Number 5
**Bottom:** Moving Day – Cabin Number 1

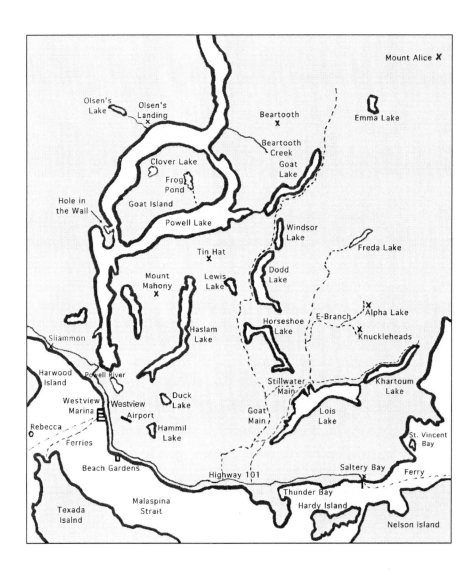

Mount Alice ✗

Olsen's Lake
Olsen's Landing ✗

Beartooth ✗

Emma Lake

Beartooth Creek

Clover Lake

Goat Lake

Frog Pond

Hole in the Wall

Goat Island

Powell Lake

Windsor Lake

Freda Lake

Tin Hat ✗

Dodd Lake

Mount Mahony ✗

Lewis Lake

Horseshoe Lake

E-Branch

✗ Alpha Lake

Haslam Lake

Knuckleheads ✗

Sliammon

Harwood Island

Powell River

Stillwater Main

Khartoum Lake

Westview Marina

Westview Airport

Duck Lake

Goat Main

Lois Lake

Rebecca ○

Hammil Lake

St. Vincent Bay

Ferries

Beach Gardens

Highway 101

Saltery Bay ✗

Ferry

Thunder Bay

Texada Island

Malaspina Strait

Hardy Island

Nelson Island

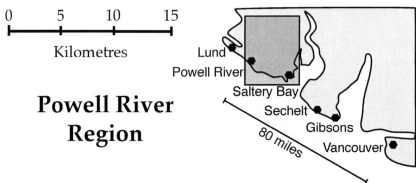

| 0 | 5 | 10 | 15 |

Kilometres

# Powell River Region

Lund
Powell River
Saltery Bay
Sechelt
Gibsons
Vancouver

80 miles

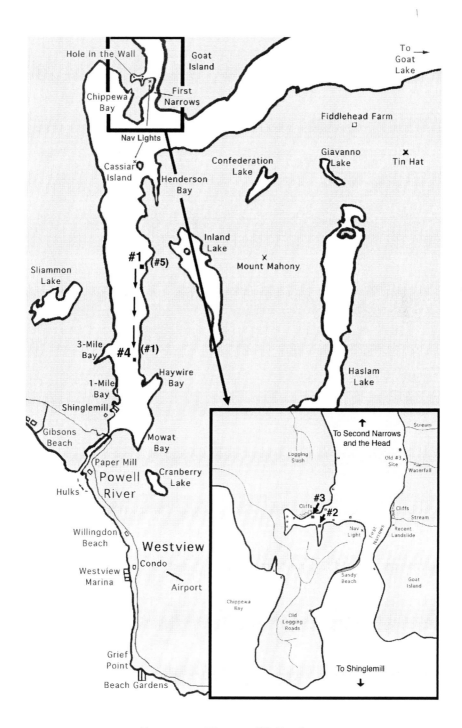

# Lower Powell Lake

# Contents

# Chapter 1

# Number 5

John numbers his floating cabins based on their order of construction. As is typical of his standards, it's a logical system. But difficult to understand from the outside looking in.

Leaving Shinglemill for a trip up the lake, the first of John's cabins is Number 4. It's little more than a placeholder of a cabin, commonly referred to as the Tool Box. It's logical that the Box is the fourth cabin constructed or rebuilt by John, although the first of his cabins you encounter on the lake.

Continuing north, Number 1 is next, the current location of most of John's projects. All of his cabins are active in their own regard, but Number 1 is where he concentrates his latest cabin building activity. Within the breakwater of Number 1, a grouping of twenty cedar logs floats loosely tied by rope, ready to form the foundation of a new cabin. Next to this future cabin sits the current Cabin Number 1.

Farther up the lake, at Hole in the Wall, is my cabin, Number 3. I bought this cabin from John ten years ago, but we still call it Number 3. And across the bay sits Number 2. It's all perfectly logical.

The numbers have now increased. For a new cabin, designated Number 5 is being born. It begins as series of float logs, hauled down Goat Lake's Frogpond Main and dropped into the water at the Clover Lake logging dock, six kilometres north of Hole in the Wall. These twenty cedar logs were then towed down the lake to temporarily rest at Number 2, then farther south where they currently sit next to Number 1. That's where John's newest cabin will be built, fifth in the line of construction.

This is the story of Number 5.

\* \* \* \* \*

While I'm in California, John tows his float foundation logs into place, inside the breakwater at Number 1. Meanwhile, I fight my way north in my Piper Arrow, sneaking into the Pacific Northwest between late September storms. The first week of October is spent in Bellingham, waiting for the latest series of low pressure troughs to move out of the area. The jet stream roars overhead, drawing autumn storms down the BC coast from the Gulf of Alaska.

There's a brief respite between the line of gales that allows me to sneak into Powell River on a solo flight that keeps me plenty busy. I'm used to the luxury of having Margy as my copilot, but she remains in Bellingham for another week. Her assistance is particularly valuable when flying under the complexity of instrument flight rules (IFR), necessitated today by the still-marginal weather conditions.

I'm fully engaged and focused on the cockpit panel during the one-hour flight to Campbell River, where I'll clear Customs. Today, in and out of clouds, it's a full-time job flying the airplane while presetting navigation radios for the next leg and keeping up with the requirements of air traffic control. During the brief periods when I break free of the clouds, I refocus outside for errant floatplane traffic that might be twisting through these big sucker holes on visual flight rules.

But by the time I pull off the runway at Campbell River, I'm back in my element. The weather is still showery, but I'll be able to complete the rest of the flight below the overcast. Clearing Customs is as simple as parking in the red box until my flight-planned estimated time of arrival, and then leaving. I'm a known traveler in the government computers, and seldom bothered by even a spot check.

By comparison to the flight from Bellingham, the twenty-minute hop across the Strait of Georgia to Powell River is a snap, because I fly this leg under visual flight rules. The landmarks are familiar, and the weather is perfect. I slip over some scattered stratus clouds near Harwood Island, and slide comfortably down final approach to Runway Zero-Nine. By the time the airplane is parked and unloaded, there's still enough daylight to take care of my chores in town and head up the lake before dark.

Since this is the only dry day in over a week, John is high in the mountains, riding his quad to Ice Lake near Mount Alfred. I have just enough time to check the mail, quickly pay a few bills, coordinate some book deliveries, buy groceries, and head up the lake before the next round of rain moves in at the end of the day.

As I load my boat at the Shinglemill, a slate-gray overcast already threatens rain. I don't want to delay getting to my cabin, but there is one important stop on the way up the lake – Cabin Number 1. I waste no time casting off from the Shinglemill. A few minutes later, I'm riding comfortably over familiar waters at the south end of the lake.

When I arrive at Number 1, I'm surprised to see the new logs already laid out in a grid, with one brow log propped up on the cedar foundation framework. The new float structure fills the entire area in front of the original Cabin Number 1. John has been busy, despite the latest storms.

\* \* \* \* \*

**M**y October arrival is greeted by one sunny day (adequate for my flight), followed by a middle-of-the night storm that brings two inches of rain. The downpour and its associated winds drive my float cabin in every direction, knocks the wood gangplank into the water, and fills the tin boat so full that I have to bail it out when I check it in the middle of the night. Near noon the following day, the vicious storm departs as quickly as it rolled in. The winds are still whipping every which way in Hole in the Wall, but the sun breaks through with a burst of rainbow against Goat Island. I ponder whether John might decide to work on his new cabin float foundation today.

I briefly consider taking the Campion down the lake to see if John is working at Number 1, but whitecaps in the Hole convince me otherwise. When this water is so tossed by wind, the lower lake is undoubtedly rough. Crossing the large open area nicknamed the North Sea would be uncomfortable. Plus, it's unlikely that John would try to salvage a half-day of work under such conditions. By 3 o'clock, it's raining again, so I stay hunkered down in my cabin.

Just before sunset, conditions have calmed enough to take the tin boat out. I gather two fishing poles and head out to see if the trout

are any more inclined to bite in early October than during the spring and summer. This year has been the worst fishing I've seen on Powell Lake, but maybe the trout season is merely late. The previous winter was the harshest I've ever seen, and the summer was late and brief. The local trout must have been adversely influenced by this abnormal year-without-summer. Besides, any excuse is a good one when it comes to going fishing.

I bring the tin boat up on-plane, battling the small waves, as I head for the waterfall on Goat Island only a kilometre north of Hole in the Wall. The falls are running strong all along this section of the island, developing quickly after the rains of the recent storm.

On my second cast into the churning water where the waterfall enters the lake, an 8-inch trout hits my red-and-white daredevil, but he gets off my line just as I'm pulling him into the boat. A few casts later, I catch a slightly larger rainbow, just off the edge of the roiling water. This is better fishing than I've seen all year.

But as is often the case in a hot spot near a waterfall, the fishing cools quickly. So I allow the boat to drift south with the gentle wind that drives it. I'm pushed steadily along the shoreline, close enough to cast nearly up against the rocks. It looks like an ideal spot for trout fishing, but I don't get a single bite.

I start the motor and switch to trolling, continuing south though First Narrows. Looking farther down the lake, the North Sea is full of whitecaps, just as expected. When I cross through the Narrows towards the navigation light on the other side, I'm hit by strong winds that are focused in this constricted passage. At trolling speed, I'm unable to control the direction of the small boat. After being turned around twice, I finally give up, reel in my line, and slap through the waves back to Hole in the Wall. It's not unsafe, but it certainly isn't comfortable. Yet it makes me feel better about not traveling down the lake today in the Campion, trying to find John.

\* \* \* \* \*

The next morning dawns clear and calm. The radio weather report indicates this will be the only day this week without rain, since another series of storms is already moving down the coast. My guess is that John will use this chance to work on Cabin Number 5. I plan to surprise him by showing up to assist.

In reality, I know there isn't a lot I can do to aid in this project, but John is always grateful for my help. Usually it's only a matter of handing him tools and keeping him company, but John always appreciates it. He's a solo worker on almost any project, and what he accomplishes by himself is amazing. For him, it's pure luxury to have an able-bodied assistant.

I don my coveralls, heavy boots, and pack a lunch. By 10:30, I'm on my way down the lake, probably well-timed to meet John just after he arrives. But when I get to Cabin Number 1, I find a few surprises.

First, John didn't beat me. The lake is in already in bright sunshine, except for the east shore where the cabin sits. I'm pretty close to Number 1 before I can tell John's boat isn't sitting in the morning's shadow. But even before I can tell his boat is absent, I see a splash right off the edge of his breakwater. It would take a mighty large fish to make a splash that big. Beating John to the cabin, a sizable fish, and now a third surprise – a second large brow log has been added to the float.

It's obvious that John was here yesterday, undoubtedly in the afternoon, after the storm passed through. Even then, it must have been a battle to travel up the lake in the winds I witnessed at Hole in the Wall. And to pull another brow log into position by himself, even with the assistance of a winch, is a feat difficult to imagine.

Maybe John is simply running late, so I cut my engine outside of his breakwater and allow my boat to drift along the boomsticks. It's a gorgeous morning, still in the shade here, looking out over the sparkling lake. And while I'm here, there's the matter of that fish.

I pull out my fishing pole, one of two I always carry with me in the Campion. I select the largest red-and-white daredevil I have, big enough to scare away a small trout. But just right for a big one.

I cast along the outer line of breakwater logs, a good spot for a trout. In just a few casts, a fish strikes my line, and the battle is on. I'm yelling and holding my pole high to try to keep this fish on the line, knowing that my barbless hook looses a lot of fish. He fights hard, but I win, hauling a fat 14-inch cutthroat trout into the boat. It may not be a monster by others' standards, but it's the biggest trout I've pulled from this lake so far, a beautiful fish.

I handle the trout carefully, pulling the hook from its mouth with a pair of pliers. The fish is still full of life and anxious to get back in the water, so I'm not worried about reviving it. The cutthroat seems ready to jump from my grasp, if I allow him to, so I simply place the fish in the water and relax my grip. The beautiful trout darts away, following a shallow arc downward. I yell in excitement, probably more thrilled with the release than the catch.

But there's no sign of John. When he awoke this morning to a rare clear day, knowing it is the last sunny day in the forecast for the next week, he probably decided to go riding on his quad. Meanwhile, I show up for my first day of work on the new float cabin, and the boss isn't there because he's goofing off. So I go fishing. In my mind, that's good employee relations. There's no question – I have a fine boss. But I'm not yet sure it's the perfect job for me.

◊ ◊ ◊ ◊ ◊ ◊

# Chapter 2

# Haulin' Cable

On a promising October morning, I drive to John's house to meet him for the trip up the lake. We'll use my boat, since it has more power, particularly valuable for today's goal of towing a raft with two 300-pound spools of three-quarter-inch steel cable to the cabin construction site. But first we need to get the raft that's stored at Cabin Number 4, two kilometres up the lake.

The front seat of John's truck is full – two people, one dog, and lots of tools. In the bed of the truck are the two spools of cable, which take nearly all of the available space. Jammed between the spools are our backpacks, two turfer winches, more tools, and enough food to keep two guys and a dog going for the day.

Our first stop is the Shinglemill Marina, where John drops me off to get the boat. While he drives over to Mowat Bay, I crank up the Campion and motor across to meet him. Just as I arrive at the dock, he pulls into Mowat, parks his truck, and gives Bro a chance for a brief run. Within a few minutes, they join me in the Campion, with the engine still running. I probably surprise John by still sitting in the driver's seat.

"Shall I drive?" I ask.

"Sure," says John, his eyebrows raised in surprise.

"Just kiddin'," I say as I slip out of the seat and wait for John to take over.

I could drive, of course, but I never do when John is aboard. It's understood by both of us that he's in command whenever we're aboard one of our boats. We both prefer it that way.

We cruise up to Number 4, hook up to the raft, and begin the slow process of towing it back to Mowat Bay.

"Five knots is about max," says John, once we settle into the tow. "See how the front of the raft is trying to dive into the water."

"Maybe we can go faster on the way back, with the spools loaded towards the back," I suggest.

"Could be, but don't expect much improvement," replies John. "Not much of a raft you know. But it gets the job done."

Which it does, as do all of John's rafts. They are strategically placed at his three float cabins, where they stand ready for almost any transport task.

A half-hour later, we pull into the Mowat dock, where a man paces back and forth, as if he's waiting for us.

"Always somebody who has to get nosey," says John. "Must not have anything else to do."

We've come to Mowat with the raft in order to avoid spectators as we load the spools. We're not doing anything wrong, but a raft and a few spools of cable can draw an inquisitive crowd. Right now, the crowd consists of one innocent passer-by who is merely interested in what's going on.

"Building something big?" says the man, as I throw him our docking line.

"A float cabin, from scratch," I reply.

The man nods in acknowledgement. People around here respect those involved in construction, especially anything big. I'm pleased to suggest I'm part of the construction crew. Maybe he even thinks I'm in charge.

"How long will it take?" he asks, maybe thinking this is a few-months project.

"Don't know. We're taking it one day at a time. Probably a couple of years."

What I don't know is how long it will really take. There's no specific time target, because that would impose significant constraints. We'll make headway as opportunities arise involving materials, weather, finances, and (of course) quad rides for the boss. John is good about waiting for bargains to appear, so we could be delayed for months waiting for sales on lumber, windows, hardware, and heavy-duty tools available for loan. In fact, though I have little concept of how long the building process will take, it will be almost three full years before we arrive at "lockup," when the cabin can finally be secured for the first time with walls, doors, and windows in place. The expensive and slowest part – waiting out bargains on interior appliances and furnishings – will take even longer.

"Got to haul some cable up the lake," I say to the man, who hangs around the raft waiting to see what's going to happen next.

Meanwhile, John retrieves his truck from the parking lot and backs it down the boat ramp. I walk the raft around the Campion, using the still-attached tow rope. It's a fairly easy task – anything that floats in the water is easy to move, just not so easy to maneuver. John hops back onto the dock to help me secure the raft, and the man lends a hand, too.

"Thanks!" says John.

John just likes to act grumpy about curious spectators. In reality, I know he appreciates the interest, just as we're always interested in what others are building.

Off-loading the spools from the truck is a tricky process. We position the raft in the shallow water, close enough to the truck so we can roll the heavy spools directly off the tailgate, but we'll need to keep the raft from bottoming out under the added weight. We slide the spools onto the raft as carefully as possible, but they still arrive with a thud. We adjust their position for proper balance by jostling them around, and then tie them to the raft, just in case the load tips.

While John takes his truck back to the parking area, I back the Campion into position. By now, our only observer has disappeared, and I await John's assistance to hook up to the raft. In just a few minutes, we're properly connected and ready to go. While John starts the Campion's engine, I shorten the tow line to allow easier maneuvering near shore. Once clear of the dock, I let the rope out to its full 50-foot extension.

The ride back up the lake is no faster than coming down. Even with the heavy cable balanced a bit rearward, the raft still plows water.

"Time to install the new radio," says John.

He relinquishes the driver's seat to me, a rarity for us, while he climbs into the rear of the boat, over our load of tools and personal gear, looking for the radio. He finds the plastic bag that contains the modified car radio, on sale at Canadian Tire, and brings it up front.

"Quite a bargain, if it works," says John.

I know it will work. After all, John has planned it out thoroughly, including the mounting plate he fashioned out of thick metal. Replacing the internally corroded marine radio with a car radio isn't normally recommended. Then again, the expensive (and supposedly waterproof) boat radio only lasted a few years. So a bargain radio, modified by John, is worth a try. Now it only needs to be installed and hooked up.

As a result of precise alterations by John, the new radio slides perfectly into the mounting bracket on the side panel of the Campion. He connects the wires, adds a rubber gasket between the metal faceplate and the side panel, and screws the radio into place.

He toggles the On switch, and loud background static blares from the speakers. But when he activates the Scan button, the tuner immediately settles on a crystal clear version of the voice of Avril Lavigne.

"Hit the preset for channel number one," I say. "That's a good station."

"How do I do that?" he asks.

"You've got to be kidding," I reply. "Just hold button number one until you hear a beep."

"Okay," he says.

He holds the button, and the radio beeps in compliance.

"You really don't know how to set stations on a car radio?" I ask.

"I never use the radio in my truck," he says. "I think it works though."

He's perfectly serious. Radios are an invention that John considers a waste of time. He goes through life without ever operating radios, and he doesn't seem any the worse for it.

We motor past Cabin Number 4 (the Tool Box), then farther north to Cabin Number 1, where the new foundation logs for Cabin Number 5 await us. John takes back control of the boat as we approach the breakwater entrance, and maneuvers the raft through the narrow opening.

We tie up three hours after we left John's house for the Shinglemill. Of course, when we return to town later today, we'll need to retrace our steps. John will retrieve his truck at Mowat Bay, while I take the Campion back to the Shinglemill, where John will pick me up. When building a cabin that floats on a lake, nothing is easy or fast.

* * * * *

**O**ur first full day of work together goes slow. After spending three hours just getting to the work site with our materials, half the day is already shot. What time remains, we use mostly for measuring and adjusting the position of the float logs.

John uses a long-handled peavy to make the protruding length of the float logs equal on each side, relative to the brow logs on top. He works this prying-and-rotating tool to slide and roll the logs. When he takes a break and leans the peavy against a brow log, it slips a few inches and then suddenly slides directly towards a gap between the logs.

"Grab it!" he yells.

But it's too late. I'm too far away, and John is at an impossible angle. In just a few seconds, the peavy hits the narrow opening between the logs and is gone, lost in 30 feet of water. Dropping tools during float construction is a constant hazard, and John is always attentive to the problem. Almost never does he loose anything into the water. But this time he has lost an extremely valuable tool, and he's terribly frustrated.

"Expensive," he says. "Probably about ninety dollars. And the water is way too cold and deep to dive without a wetsuit and a tank. I won't be able to get it back until next summer."

I feel for him. John protects his property carefully, and I'd never expect him to loose a tool, especially one as valuable as this. Yet it has happened on one of our first workdays on the float. It's a bad omen.

From my standpoint, the only positive factor is that I'm not to blame. It could happen so easy, and I'd be devastated if I was responsible for losing John's peavy. I have the feeling this won't be the only tool lost during the construction process, and it's most likely that I'll hold the record – not an enviable forecast.

The rule of thumb for float cabin living is to never drop anything on the outside the cabin, especially near the edges of the deck. Even with the small cracks between deck boards, things find their way to these openings. Hang onto your keys, and pass things from person to person carefully. When working on a float foundation of logs, with much bigger "cracks," hold onto tools and materials with both hands, whenever possible. And never drop anything on the "floor" that's big enough to fall through a gap in the logs (sometimes as large as 6 inches). Even a big tool, like a peavy, can turn sideways and immediately hone in on a gap between logs, disappearing forever. The proof today is provided by the master of the don't-lose-it philosophy, John himself.

We try to get back to work, but John is dogged by his momentary carelessness. He mutters to himself about his negligence throughout the afternoon. Now he uses a pike pole in place of the peavy, but it provides less leverage and isn't suitable for rolling logs. On one log, he pries a little too hard, and the end-hook breaks off the pike pole. It can be repaired, but the incident mars the day even further.

We use three winches to adjust the float platform, trying to keep the logs in alignment in preparation for the final cable stitching that's still days away. In just a few hours, the float is nearly square. We'll leave the winches in place until the float is tightly sewn together.

Most of today's remaining time is spent with adjustments to the log overhang dimensions. We move the logs into temporary position, then use spray paint to mark their alignment against one of the brow logs.

Once, when adjusting the distance between the two brow logs, I drop the tape measure. Nearly panicked over adding to John's woes of the day, I reach down nearly instantaneously and grab the end of the tape, just as the reel disappears through a gap in the logs. I hang on for dear life.

"You lost the tape!" yells John, who misses absolutely nothing, even from the far side of the float.

"I've still got it," I reply, trying to keep my voice under control.

My grip on the end of the tape is precarious, barely between my thumb and finger. But my grasp is determined, and finally I'm able to reach down and hold the end more securely with my other hand. Then I start to slowly pull the now-unwound tape up through the water. I just hope it isn't wrapped around a rock or other snag on the bottom.

By now, John is hovering over me, making me even more nervous.

"You're not going to get it back," he says, offering minimal encouragement.

"I won't lose it," I counter, gritting my teeth and pulling slowly on the tape.

The long, flexible tape inches upward, until finally I feel the full weight of the reel coming up. I've got it!

"We need to be more careful," says John, as the reel reappears in the gap between the logs.

It's an understatement, of course, but he's criticizing himself as much as me. I'm grateful I've retrieved the tape and haven't lost anything during my first day on the job – yet.

By now, a light rain has begun. But it's warm and not unpleasant working conditions, so we continue for another hour. We adjust the position of a few more logs and paint some more the alignment marks. Then we stop to admire our progress. A few of the logs have already shifted out of position, but the marks will allow us to easily readjust them before sewing the logs together with the steel cable. Maybe more importantly, these small white marks make us realize we are making progress, slow but sure.

◊ ◊ ◊ ◊ ◊ ◊ ◊

# Chapter 3

# Diagonals and Parallelograms

The next work day, I drive the Campion down the lake from my cabin at Hole in the Wall to meet John at the float construction site. He waves me into a precarious spot at the end of the float. Comfortable tie-up space is limited, and John's boat occupies the only almost-permanent docking location. I throw him a rope, and he secures it to the brow log.

With the winches now holding the logs loosely in formation, walking on the float logs is more stable but still cumbersome. It's a process of carefully stepping from log-to-log, with each stride fighting a slightly different gap between logs and a different log height. The walking pace is uneven, and some of the float logs begin to roll if I remain on them too long. Our workplace has a floor that is rough and irregular, and we'll be walking on that shifting foundation for a long time during the initial construction.

Our main task today is to weave the steel cable around one of the brow logs, preparing it for eventual stitching and tightening of the float. But first we need to pull all of the cable off the spool and run it out as straight as possible, so it will wind onto the brow log properly.

It takes both of us to pull the cable from the reel and drag it to its full length. We use the bridge to shore to straighten it, running the cable up the pathway past the outhouse. The 300 feet of three-quarter-inch steel cable follows the cliff trail all the way to the gravel beach. Together we untwist the remaining coils, a process that seems

impossible for one person. Yet I know John is used to working by himself on such projects, and routinely handles multi-person tasks without assistance. How he does it, I'm not sure.

With the cable nearly straight, we begin the process of weaving it under the first float log and then up and over the brow log. Then we angle the cable back down into the water, below the next float log, and upward again over the brow log. It's like sewing a seam, but the cloth is made of logs and the thread of heavy steel cable.

Each time we connect another log, we need to pull more cable from shore. Like a needle and thread, you move ahead one stitch at a time. In a few hours, we progress halfway across the float. On another day, we'll return to the stitching with a hydraulic jack, to tighten each of the braids, one log at a time. Then we'll do the same for the other brow log.

While we thread the cable into position, Malcom arrives unexpectedly on his jet ski. In a sad note regarding the change of seasons, he's on his last ride of the year, burning off his tank of anti-contamination fuel in preparation for winter storage.

"Look!" I yell to John. "He's wearing a wet suit."

John laughs, knowing what I have in mind. But it's too deep to go down for the lost peavy without an air tank, even with a wet suit. Still we kid Malcom about it.

"You can do it," says John. "We'll haul you back up, if you turn into an ice-cube."

Malcom assists with the stitching process, allowing us to speed through the rest of the brow log. A third set of hands helps a lot, and within another hour we have completed the loose weaving of the cable on the first brow log. Bro, John's black Lab, also helps, providing dog-critical supervision of our work.

After Malcom leaves, blasting away on his jet ski (demonstrating a maximum acceleration departure at my request), we turn to the final tweaking of the float. All logs are in place, but the dimensions aren't perfectly square. The two diagonal measurements are off by nearly a metre, indicating a parallelogram shape that's impossible to distinguish from a rectangle at a glance. But such imprecision would cause havoc with final squaring of the structure. So we make more measurements and repeated adjustments to gaps between the logs.

We use a turfer winch to slide the brow logs across the float logs, evening up the sides. Once the brow logs are tightened, there'll be no further opportunity. But the diagonal measurements keep going astray. It's easy enough to adjust the cant of the float with a slight tightening tug with the turfer, but it's also easy to overshoot. We make repeated measurements, checking and rechecking, and begin to get a little punchy.

"What was that last diagonal?" asks John.

"Fifty-five feet, seven inches," I think.

"Let's do it again."

So we do it again, and again, tweaking the winches until the float is within inches of square in all dimensions. When it comes to one final adjustment, I crawl out onto the end of the brow log and reach down to attach a choke cable to the end-most float log. We'll fasten a turfer here, adjusting it to that all-perfect setting. I get a little sloppy, and lay the end of the choker down on the log, while I stretch out on my belly and reach underwater to grab the other end of the short cable. It takes just a second – the cable is gone!

I lay motionless on the brow log, waiting for reality to sink in. This is another valuable piece of equipment, not readily replaceable. And I have lost it to a watery grave.

"What's going on?" yells John, when I don't move for quite a while. "Can't you find the end of the choker?"

Silence. Then: "John, you're going to be really mad at me."

More prolonged silence.

"You lost it, didn't you?"

"I dropped it. John, I'm really sorry."

Silence.

"Oh, well," he says with a weak voice of sadness. "I guess we better think about hiring somebody to go down under the float and just stay there while we drop expensive stuff into the water."

That's one way to look at it.

We finish the job, finally squaring off the float by using a rope to replace the choke cable. It isn't the best way to do it, but it works. With the silver-coloured braiding cable spread around the brow log, there are visible signs of progress. But we've got to stop dropping stuff before we run out of tools, materials, and patience.

# Chapter 4

# In the Rain

The day after we wind the cable on the first brow log (still not tightened), the first of a series of storms moves in. October troughs line up off the coast, coming ashore one after the other with barely a break between storms. To add to this delay, John comes down with a cold that disables him for a week. When he finally feels well enough to work, another low pressure system is moving in.

As the latest storm begins to roll onshore, Margy and I are trying to get out of town and up the lake before the wind begins. But the morning drags out in a series of seemingly endless errands, including last minute email projects, a visit to the lumber store, and shopping for a few essentials at the grocery store. By the time I push our buggy of food to the truck, the rain is already falling. But the wind is still only light. We should be able to beat the storm up the lake.

At the Shinglemill, Margy and I load the boat quickly and are on our way. The lower lake cooperates, as we maneuver along our standard route along the east shoreline, a course that better protects us from developing storm winds (typically from the southeast). This route also allows us to check the security of John's cabins as we progress up the lake. Number 4 with its placeholder floating shed is first. Number 1 with the new float for Number 5 is next.

When the round the point near Number 1, I can see John's boat tucked in against the new float foundation. Since he hates working in the rain and is supposedly still sick, this is a bit of a mystery.

"The weather's holding pretty well," I say to Margy as we maneuver into the breakwater entrance. "If John can use my assistance today, I'd like to offer to help."

"Sure," she replies. "I don't mind waiting."

Margy and I have come to an agreement about this project. She wants to be involved in the construction of Cabin Number 5, but the developing float is still a rough obstacle course for a person who doesn't feel sure-footed, and Margy is quick to admit her lack of balance on the logs. When we eventually start installing the deck, the walking surface will be much more stable, and she'll be able to help with the project then. But for now, she should stay off the new float. Fortunately, she's good about waiting for almost anything. And her backpack always contains plenty of reading material.

"You can take the boat up to the cabin, and come back and get me later," I suggest.

"Waste of gas," she says. "I'll just stay."

John is glad to see us, especially when he finds out I'm willing to assist with cabling up the second brow log. But he's reluctant to accept my offer.

"You're not dressed for it," he says. "At least I'm wearing raingear."

True. My slipper shoes aren't ideal for working on the logs, and I don't want to get my favourite jacket dirty. But this should be fairly clean work, since the cable is new, and my shoes won't be unsafe for the task.

"I can still help," I say. "This jacket will handle a little rain, and Margy doesn't mind waiting. She can keep Bro occupied while we work."

Bro is a bit of a problem in conditions like these. He refuses to come in out of the rain, preferring to hang out near John and get wet rather than sneak under cover. But with Margy here, he'll be glad to keep her company inside Cabin Number 1.

"I've got a fire going," says John, nodding towards the cabin. "And look what I've just done to the spool of cable."

I glance at the raft that holds the new cable, and notice something that I should have seen when I arrived. The spool is now balanced on its side, raised off the raft by the other empty spool and a log, with a

rod through the center. Rather than drag all of the cable off the reel in advance, as we did for the first brow log, we should be able to peel off the cable as needed.

John walks a plank to the raft and prepares the cable for unwinding. This should work well, but I'm amazed that John was able to lift the spool of heavy cable into position all by himself.

John hands me the end of the cable, and asks me to begin pulling. Sure enough, while he guides the spool to make sure it's steady, the cable rolls off easily. In fact, it rolls too well. If you pull too hard, the spool speeds too fast, unwinding cable that drops deep into the water. As more cable drops downward, the added weight causes the spool to spin faster, careening out of control.

"You need to pull at just the right speed," John instructs. "Once you get used to it, it'll be easy.

He's right. I get used to the pull that's needed to keep the cable coming, without dropping too much into the water. In a few minutes we're working our way through the float logs, weaving the cable around them and over the brow log at a fairly rapid pace. The improved cable feed from the spool is a muscle-saver, and within an hour we're halfway across the float, working in a continuous light rain that's beginning to soak through my non-waterproof jacket and go-to-town pants.

"We'll need to jam these logs apart," says John, pointing to a place where there's almost no gap. "I can insert wood blocks to keep the spacing between them wide enough. Otherwise, the cable will get snagged."

While John works on another stitch, I hunt wooden chunks to shove between the logs. As we work farther outward, these blocks will become increasingly important, as the logs tighten against each other in a self-induced attempt to keep the float's rectangular shape. A small snatch-block winch is roped to the log at the outside end, holding the float square until we can tighten the brow cables. We can loosen the winch a little, but we don't want to lose the symmetrical shape we've already achieved.

Bro hears me rummaging for wood near the cabin, and comes out to see what's going on. As I retrieve some blocks stacked on the cabin's deck, Bro watches intently, and then follows me back out onto the new float.

On the way back, carrying an awkwardly balanced pile of blocks, I do the impossible. I step between two logs, lose my balance, and fall forward. The space between the logs is currently only a few inches, but the weight of my body in the gap somehow manages to force the logs apart far enough to engulf both of my feet. I slam down into the water between the logs until my hips stop the descent. I'm unhurt, but my legs dangle below the float in cold October water.

"What in the world?" exclaims John as he hears me crash down between the logs.

Within a few seconds he's standing beside me to assist, but I have already worked myself upward until only my lower legs are under water, my ankles locked by a log on each side. I sit down on the float, knees bent, unable to extract my feet from the wooden vise.

"We'll need your chainsaw to cut off my feet," I say.

"Don't kid around!" says John. "Are you okay?"

"No problem. Just can't get my feet out."

I wiggle around, while John pries the logs apart with a pike pole. My feet come out just fine, but my shoes, socks, and pants are soaked.

Since we've been working in a light rain for over an hour, the rest of my body isn't much drier.

"We'll need to get you out of those shoes, and find some dry pants," says John.

"Actually, I'm not cold," I say. "Just a bit squishy in the feet. I can keep going until we finish this cable."

I'm pretty good about taking care of myself, and I know there's risk of getting thoroughly chilled now that I'm soaked. But the air is warm, and my feet aren't cold in my thick, wet socks, plus there's heated warmth in the cabin if I need it. So I decide to continue.

We go back to work. I walk across the logs with a *squish-squish* in my shoes, while John reiterates his surprise that anyone could fall through the gap in the logs.

"I just can't believe it. How did you do that?"

"Good aim," I reply.

We make our way through the remaining stitches of cable, finishing off with multiple loops around each end of the brow log. It's a strange job to tackle on a rainy day, but we've finished the initial cabling of the second brow log. Besides, if you don't work in the rain during the autumn, you might not work at all.

# Chapter 5

# Number 1 through 4

Depending on how you count, John has already built (or rebuilt) at least four cabins. His talent for building things was probably first expressed when he began building forts as a youngster in the Kootenays, when he lived with his parents in Fruitvale. At the age of 12, along with his older brother, Dave, he constructed a 6-foot square tree fort in a tamarack tree. Together with another of his brothers, Rick, John constructed a land-based cabin behind their house. Though only 8-feet by 10-feet in footprint, it was a more traditional dwelling. Not to be outdone by conventional designs, he then progressed to an underground floorplan – a cave-like fort complete with trenches, and covered by dirt and wood.

When John, age 15, moved to Powell River with his family, their new home didn't include enough acreage to accommodate any cabins, so John moved his construction activities to nearby Haslam Lake where he and Rick built an 8-foot by 10-foot cabin halfway up the lake on the north side. His skills were getting more elaborate now, but it took a boat to get to the construction site. As usual, the real thrill for John was in the building phase rather than the live-in-it process. His goal was met, and he moved on.

This construction history predated my discovery of Powell Lake in 2000, and John never talked much about his cabin accomplishments. In fact, I often had to pry information out of his modest mind. But every time I did get a glimpse of that history, I learned something new and interesting. Thus, when I finally got a chance to drill him on the details, I took full advantage.

\* \* \* \* \*

**O**ne August night, at our campsite at the head of Powell Lake, John and I settle in for some meteor watching. The Perseids Meteor Shower is only two days away from peak, and this should be a good night for dark-sky observing, considering the lack of moonlight and the clarity of the evening. While the twilight is inching towards total darkness, we sit on the boat dock next to our quads, a riding adventure come true. We've been talking about hauling a raft with our quads aboard to the Head for years. Now we're finally here.

After our first day of riding, we're tired, but well fed. John brings out the potato chips that serve as our dessert, and we sit and talk, awaiting the meteors. I pull out my digital tape recorder, smaller than a mini-camera, and set it on the dock in front of us. John looks at it suspiciously.

"You don't mind if I record this, do you?" I ask.

"Record what?" he asks with a suspicious tone.

"It's just a tape recorder. I need to get some background about the cabins you built before I knew you – for my new book about Cabin Number 5. It's a lot easier to record than take notes. Okay?"

"Guess so. But what don't you know?"

"Well, I'd like to know more about your background in building cabins, especially those on Powell Lake."

Thus, our conversation begins. As usual, what I learn is filled with a few surprises.

\* \* \* \* \*

**"S**o how did you get interested in constructing cabins on the lake?" I ask. "You can't even see float cabins from the bottom of the lake where the roads end."

"When I was in high school, Dad had a houseboat, and we'd spend lots of time up the lake. So I saw what was there, and thought I'd like to try building something. At the time, there weren't any rules about it. You just went in and started building wherever you wanted. No water leases, no taxes, nothing to worry about.

"Dave and I built the first cabin in his backyard, just an experiment really. He had just bought a house, and I found a bunch of old two-by-fours. Scrounged some 45-gallon metal barrels."

"Metal, not plastic like today's blue barrels?" I ask.

"The barrels were the cabin foundation, rather than cedar. No brow logs – just metal barrels that I welded together with angle iron in Dave's yard, like a pontoon. Turned out to be as unstable as hell."

"We towed it down to the lake on Dad's houseboat trailer, still in pieces. The walls sat down flat on the trailer, and we raised them once we got up the lake."

"Up the lake, where?" I ask.

"We picked a spot directly across from where Number 5 is now. About where that rental cabin is today. Put it together there. Flat roof, no real deck, except some wood sticking out on the front and back, nothing on the sides. It was freaky – when boats went by, it bobbed like a cork."

"So it was pretty tiny? And unstable."

"Ten-by-twelve, with plywood walls. So wobbly that you really couldn't stay overnight. Dave and I tried it once, since we'd installed bunk beds. He had the top bunk and had to tie himself in with a rope so he wouldn't fall out."

"Now that's wobbly!"

"Later we added some boomsticks on the side, which helped a lot. Kinda' like outriggers. But then we pretty well blew it off – lost interest and just left it there, until I came back, and Fritz had taken it over."

"Fritz? You mean the Fritz of Three-Mile Bay?"

"Yuh. He was new to the lake then, and found our cabin. It was pretty deteriorated by then, so he started taking the walls down, and used the platform to set up a tent."

"So what did you do?"

"Well, there was a bit of a confrontation. I said: 'Hey, buddy, this is my bloody float and my spot.' And I remember his exact words."

"Which were?..."

"If you neglect, I collect."

That sure sounds like Fritz.

"But he took his stuff and left," says John. "And I used the spot to build Number 1."

\* \* \* \* \*

John purchased the float foundation that was to become Cabin Number 1 when he was only 20 years old, probably the youngest cabin owner on the lake. At the time, he had a new job at the paper mill, and came up with the $1000 needed to buy an old float that was sitting in Haywire Bay.

"It was in pretty bad shape, with trees growing on it like some of the old floats you see at logging docks. But I took it to Mowat Bay and ripped out the trees. Several other float cabins were being built at Mowat at the time. I'd watch other guys building their floats there, putting on brow logs and installing cables. Learned a lot just by watching."

"So back then, you could just go to Mowat and start building? Needed to get permission from somebody, I suppose."

"No, didn't need permission. You'd just do it, and nobody said anything. At the time, most of the cabins on the lake were owned by guys from the mill, and there really weren't any rules to worry about."

From Mowat Bay, John towed the float to the spot where the old barrel float was located, and began constructing the cabin.

"Dad helped a lot, both with the labor and ideas for the design. We'd talk things over as we built, changing as we went along. In less than a year, we had the exterior complete. Then I towed it across to where Cabin Number 5 is now. 'Course, I don't call it that."

"You mean you don't call it 'Cabin Number 5.'"

"Well, sometimes I do, because you do. But usually I just call it 'the new cabin.' Can't really call it Number 1, because Number 1 is down at Number 4 now."

It gets complicated, but I still call it Number 5.

"We finished the interior within another year. Worked out pretty good."

\* \* \* \* \*

John negotiated a reasonable deal with a friend at the paper mill, which resulted in his next cabin, Number 2, but it needed a complete renovation. This cabin site at Hole in the Wall is one of the most picturesque small bays on the lake, directly across from my current cabin (Number 3).

For the reconstruction project, John towed the cabin to Kinsman's Beach, adjacent to the Shinglemill. While completely gutting the cabin and installing new brow logs and cables, John found old studs that were dated *1944*. His brother, Rick, helped with the renovations, including installation of a new roof. Then they towed the cabin back to Hole in the Wall for completion of the interior.

John began renting Number 2, along with Number 1, and was ready to move on to a third cabin. His construction efforts were really a goal within themselves, but renting gave it an official purpose, which could more properly be considered an excuse.

\* \* \* \* \*

Cabin Number 3 began as a logging company float, and John converted it into my present and beloved home. The brow logs were too small for John's needs, so he replaced them during the initial phase of construction adjacent to Cabin Number 1.

"It had been used as a work float, with choppers landing on it to carry off shake blocks from Goat Island. Dad and Rick helped me right from the beginning, and construction moved along pretty fast."

"When we finished the exterior, I towed the cabin to Chippewa Bay, but that didn't work out. The water was way too rough, even in the summer. I'd go up there when I was working on the kitchen, and the waves would be rocking everything silly. So I moved it over to Goat Island."

This location, near Hole in the Wall, is next to a stream and waterfall. John had hopes of harnessing the stream for water and electrical power, but his stay there was short. After only a few weeks, he decided that passing tugs and their barges (and log booms) came too close to the cabin. If you're going to have a private cabin, it shouldn't be on the main highway.

Thus, my cherished home found it's final spot on Powell Lake. And I plan to never move it again.

✶ ✶ ✶ ✶ ✶

"So you built Number 3 primarily for rental, didn't you?" I ask.

"Yes, but I never rented it much before you bought it from me."

"That's not what I've heard. It seems like everyone I talk to says they rented Number 3 at one time or the other."

"People like to brag a lot," replies John.

"Well, Number 3 is worth bragging about."

"But they probably get it confused with Number 2, which I rented a lot more often."

"Which brings us to Number 4," I remind him.

"The Tool Box," he says.

"Right. You built it as a place-holder."

"I claimed the spot before the government moved in and started telling us where we could go. I put the Tool Box there because I knew that spot would be worth some money someday. And I was right."

"But now the Tool Box is at Number 5," says John.

"I thought you called Number 5 'the new cabin.'"

"You know what I mean."

Yes, I do. Here's the real order as you come up the lake: Number 4 (which now holds Cabin Number 1), Number 5 (which used to be Number 1), then Number 2, and finally Number 3 (which is my cabin). It's all perfectly logical.

◊ ◊ ◊ ◊ ◊ ◊

# Chapter 6

# Blueprints of the Mind

With the cable on both brow logs strung, the demanding project of tightening and securing the cable lies ahead. This is a two-person job, with each cable section tightened in sequence with a hydraulic jack, log-to-log. It's a slow process that I've witnessed before, while assisting John with refurbishment of the float foundation at Steve's cabin. The cable is pulled tight with the jack, by forcing it up from the top of the brow log; then the cable is spiked in place before moving to the next log.

Luck being what it is, I leave for a brief stay in the States just as an unexpected spell of clear weather moves into Powell River. I take advantage of the high pressure that settles over the entire Pacific Northwest, to fly my Piper Arrow south to Bellingham, then down the coast into Oregon for a highly-touted college football game (USC vs. Oregon – the good guys lose). After several days of perfect flying conditions in late October, I slip back into Powell River on the outgoing edge of the weather window. Soon after I push the Arrow back into it's hangar, the rain begins.

While I've been gone, John has completed the tightening of both brow log cables, a two-person process that he somehow performs by himself. The stitching of the logs, a major task in the construction of a float, is now complete. I try to imagine how John could have accomplished this demanding feat by himself.

"It took me four straight days," says John. "Nearly killed me."

Once he began tightening the cable, it had to be completed as quickly as possible. Otherwise logs could shift in the wind and waves, difficult to move back into position once part of the float is tightened. John tackled the entire project single-handed and with relentless perseverance. And now the float is secure for as long as it takes to build the cabin on top. The new float can bob around endlessly next to Cabin Number 1 without risk of further shifting of the foundation logs.

John is anxious to get on with the cabin construction, but we'll need to slow down for a while, tending to other projects. The next major phase, the construction of "pony walls" that raise the cabin and its surrounding deck above the float, will require lots of lumber.

Of course, this all requires money, and John is now working long hours on a variety of construction projects in town, including the building of a carport, to earn money so we can proceed. During the few good-weather days, he's confined to work in town, when we'd both rather be working on the new cabin.

⊦   In the meantime, John crawls under my cabin at Hole in the Wall, checking the design of his most recent float cabin. Since he constructs entirely with blueprints-of-the-mind, he uses memories of his previous work and after-construction inspections to guide him in the design of his new cabin.

"I'll never be able to build my new cabin as well as this one," he says, as he slips out from beneath the deck at Cabin Number 3. "The pony walls are all yellow cedar down here."

"Skookum," I reply. "This is the best cabin in the whole world."

I really believe it, but I didn't realize the foundation walls were yellow cedar.

"Way too expensive though," he states. "Couldn't afford it these days, so it'll have to be red cedar."

My cabin sits on a lumber gold mine, and I'm grateful. Yellow cedar lasts longer than the typical red cedar found at lower elevations, and it's a rare termite-proof wood.

\* \* \* \* \*

John's dad, Ed, has a new design weapon. With a new computer in the house, he uses his artistic talents along with basic drafting software to construct virtual cabins of varying design. I sit on the couch in the den at John's house, looking over Ed's shoulder as he creates a complete float with a new cabin on top. John stands beside me, watching with cautious skepticism.

"Good design, Dad," he says. "But too complex."

"Doesn't matter," says Ed. "You'll just do it your own way, anyhow."

He's right. John designs in his mind. That's where his blueprints are, and that's how the cabin will develop.

\* \* \* \* \*

With the float complete, the next step involves getting set for construction of the pony walls, raised beams that will bring the cabin and its deck above the brow logs. This step will involve a lot of lumber, and a considerable amount of cutting, shimming, and nail pounding. But before that can begin, tools and materials must be positioned at Cabin Number 1. For most independent builders, that simply means hauling a few truck-beds of material to the construction site. For John, it means a crisscross journey up and down the lake, into and out of trucks and boats. When it comes to construction, nothing is simple on the lake.

To haul the first main supply of materials and equipment (a mere pickup truck load) requires a total of six trips on the lake and an equal number of short jaunts on the land. John enjoys planning out the intricate web of transportation paths needed to accomplish the task, and I'm pleased to be a part of it. For two guys who avoid heavy lifting when at all possible, we manage to haul this first load in and out of boats and trucks a total of four times in the process.

My part of the journey begins with an early trip down the lake in the Bayliner. It's the boat of choice for today's mission, with its wide aft deck and roomy cabin that should allow the first full load of materials and equipment to be hauled in a single trip to Cabin Number 1. Now that winter is approaching, the Bayliner is docked at Cabin Number 3, removed from its normal summer habitat on the chuck. For the next 7 months, it will serve as an alternate source of transportation on the lake when major storms blow through the South Coast.

I dock at the Shinglemill, since only momentary moorage is allowed at Mowat Bay where we plan to load the boat. Then I drive to John's house, climb into John's truck (along with Bro, of course), and we drive to Doug's forested acreage, where we've temporarily stored the lumber we need to transport.

After loading the truck at Doug's (a muddy spot, so we have to rake over our deep tire ruts as we exit), John drops me off at the Shinglemill. I quickly untie the Bayliner and motor over to Mowat Bay.

As I round the end of the boom at Block Bay, I shouldn't be surprised to see John's truck already parked at the Mowat ramp, but I once again marvel at his spooky ability to always beat me to any destination by land or by sea.

We off-load the truck and pile the boards into the Bayliner, leaving a small under-lumber opening on the aft deck for Bro. Then off we go for Cabin Number 1.

Our load is so heavy that the boat won't come up on-plane. So John sends me to the bow to balance the weight. Gradually, he coaxes the Bayliner into cruise configuration, and ten minutes later we're approaching the breakwater of Number 1.

Off-loading the boat would normally require hauling everything across the new float, up onto the deck of Number 1, and then around the existing cabin to the bridge to shore, in order to reach our storage location for the construction materials. But today, with such a heavy load, we maneuver around the front of the new float, past several rows of breakwater logs that crowd against the float. I take a position in the bow, using a pike pole to push logs aside as John eases the boat through the narrow opening. In a few minutes, we're past the logjam and parked near the bridge to shore.

Now we can haul the lumber out of the boat and carry it across the bridge. Finally we're finished with the process of getting this first big load to the construction site. But we're far from done, since now everything has to be exercised in reverse to get both John and I home. There's no time today for doing much more than getting this first batch of lumber to the work site.

By late afternoon, we're back at Mowat Bay, where I drop John off at his truck. Before he and Bro hop out onto the dock, we plan things out for tomorrow.

"If you need me tomorrow, I'll come down the lake for another load," I offer.

"Sure, but we won't need your boat for that. We can fit what remains in my Hourston, so things should be easier."

Still, it will be back-and-forth all day long to deliver another load.

"See you in the morning," I say, as John kicks my stern out away from the dock. "Is ten o'clock okay?"

"How about nine?" says John.

"Okay, boss," I yell, as I shift into reverse and back away from the dock.

What a slave driver.

I round the log boom at Block Bay and head for the fuel pumps at the Shinglemill, the Bayliner riding nearly on fumes. It's too late to go back up the lake, with the late November sunset already in progress. As I slow to enter the fueling area, it suddenly dawns on me: I'm stranded here without a vehicle that can get me back to town. And

I don't have my cell phone. I should have told John to pick me up. Obviously, based on our conversation a few minutes ago at Mowat Bay, we both forgot that I would end up here without a car.

After pumping over 200 litres into the Bayliner's tanks, I ask the fuel attendant if I can leave the boat here a few minutes while I make a telephone call.

"Sure," she replies. "Nothin' goin' on today."

The launch ramp and fueling area are empty on this cold evening, as I walk to the pay phone outside the pub. If you know me, you know about my terrible attitude towards telephones. I hate them in the best of circumstances. And pay phones are even worse.

As I step into the glass enclosure, I face a distasteful-looking antiquated device. This won't go well, and I know it. Instructions on the phone say: *Insert coins, enter number.* Of course, a pay phone means coins, which I don't have. But before going back to the boat for my wallet, I decide to try dialing Margy's cell number to see what happens. I've never used a pay phone in Canada (and seldom in the States), but maybe I can use a credit card, which I have in my miniature author's notebook in my pocket.

I try dialing the number, area code first. I try dialing without the area code. I try dialing zero. Twice I get a recording that takes me though a series of menus before I hear a distinct *click*. On two other tries, I get a live voice, both times with the same annoying *click*.

"This is the operator. How may I help you?"

"I'd like to make a call…" *Click*, and then silence.

I go back to the boat, find my wallet, and try again. Nothing on the instructions posted in the booth tells me how many coins to insert. So I start with fifty cents. Three more times, once with an operator – I finish each attempt with another agonizing *click*. Finally, after wasting most of the coins in my wallet, I slam the phone back into its holder. If it isn't already broken, it will be now.

Trying to calm myself, I glance around to make sure no one has seen my telephone booth rage. There, parked only a few metres away, sits John's truck, with John inside and Bro's familiar profile next to him. The dog is looking directly away from me, as if in disgust at such a human outpouring of lack of control.

"John!" I yell. "You've saved me."

John calmly rolls down his window and gives me a inquisitive look.

"What are you doing?" he asks.

"I've been trying to use that damn phone! How long have you been here?"

"Quite a while. Just waitin' for you. I watched you gas up and go to the pay phone. Then I pulled over here and waited."

"So why didn't you tell me you were here? I've been fighting with that phone. Can't get it to work at all."

"I know. That telephone hasn't worked for months. It's worthless."

"And you just let me fight with it?"

"Figured you knew I was here, so I was just waitin' for you to finish."

"But you didn't remember I needed a ride when I dropped you off at Mowat, did you?"

"Sure. I knew you didn't have a car. So I drove right over."

Four trips by land, five by water, and one needless argument with a pay phone. Nothing is simple when you're hauling stuff on the lake.

# Chapter 7

# Pony Walls and Blue Barrels

Just before I'm scheduled to return to the States, I nurse a very sore foot. The cause isn't my episode falling between the logs at Number 5. Instead, I cut my ankle badly on a whirling fanbelt pulley in the engine compartment of the Bayliner. How does one get their foot in there in the first place? – Leave it to me to find a way.

The flight in the Piper Arrow from Powell River to Bellingham with a sore foot is the easiest part of the journey. Pushing the airplane around upon arrival at the self-serve fuel pumps (and then into the tiedown spot) takes its toll. The next day, my ankle appears to be further inflamed, so I visit a doctor. He puts me on antibiotics, and soon thereafter on crutches. I'm confined to my condo in Bellingham for over two weeks.

My recovery is excruciatingly slow, but finally I'm on my feet again and on my way back to Canada. In the meantime, John keeps me up to date over the phone regarding his progress on the float. He's working by himself building pony walls, the wooden framework that sits on top of the cedar log float foundation to support the cabin and its surrounding deck.

"I'll be there to help, as soon as I can walk again," I promise.

"No hurry," replies John. "There'll be lots to do when you get here."

Construction of a float cabin is a slow process, especially when you're doing most of it entirely by yourself, as John is. I'm anxious to get back to the lake, where I can take up a hammer and begin to build pony walls or whatever John feels he can trust me with.

* * * * *

Back in Canada in mid-February, with a foot that's fully operational again (but staying away from the rub of high-top boots), I motor up the lake for the first time in over two weeks. My first stop is the construction site at Cabin Number 1 (uhm, Number 5). The amount of progress John has attained all by himself is amazing. Sturdy wooden pony walls rise from two logs that John has added inboard of the brow logs. These open-truss walls outline the floor boundaries of the cabin, a 24-foot square box marked by the freshly cut wooden four-by-fours. More pony walls will eventually be needed to support the surrounding deck, but already the cabin's foundation is starting to grow.

Since my foot is still not healed adequately to fit comfortably into a boot, John continues to work by himself. Finally my first day back

on the job arrives, but early morning fog in Hole in the Wall delays my departure for the lower lake. I've fought fog in a boat before, and it has often been frustrating. Going south, I'll have to cross the North Sea, an area particularly prone to extensive fog during the winter. John will have an easier trip coming up the lower lake from town.

"I'm leaving now," he tells me over the phone. "But the fog will slow you down. Get there when you can."

* * * * *

**I** bandage up my foot and put on my boots for the first time in almost a month. I practice walking around my cabin deck, and I don't even feel the wound binding in my boot. Now I only need to wait for the fog to lift.

By 11 am, the fog at Hole in the Wall seems to be dissipating. I can now see Max's cabin at the entrance to the Hole. I'm anxious to get going, so I warm up the Bayliner for the trip south. The diesel heater starts with its normal cloud of grey smoke. This morning, with not even a breeze, the smoke engulfs the entire boat. Finally, the heater

kicks in, with it's *puff-puff-puff* spurt of diesel smoke that finally settles down to a nearly invisible train of exhaust.

I doubt that the area south of First Narrows is adequate for passage yet, but I have my GPS standing by, and my knowledge of Powell Lake's shoreline (at least in the lower portions) has become increasingly adequate. But though I'm comfortable dead reckoning across the North Sea relative to navigation, I'm less comfortable with the prospect of other boats sharing this section of the lake. The North Sea is the confluence of boats from three different directions, and some of them are small craft like mine without radar. Even though the big crew boats have radar, I'm not confident they'll be able to identify my fiberglass boat on their radar screens.

Crossing the North Sea in zero visibility isn't worth the chance. But once on the other side, I'll be able to navigate close to the shoreline, out of the way of faster boats. I have time on my side, so I decide to depart from the Hole and see what happens when I reach the open stretch of water beyond First Narrows. My plan, if Cassiar Island isn't visible to the south, is to simply wait it out in the Bayliner. I bring along a book, just in case.

I push off from the dock at the cabin, driving the Bayliner at minimum power. The lake is extraordinarily low, so the threat of flotsam is minimal. Still, in low visibility, logs can pop up in front of you too quickly to avoid – another reason for a slow speed in these conditions.

First Narrows is no better than the Hole, so I creep southward past the green navigation light in idle. I pass the protruding stumps at Sandy Beach, and then deviate to the right to follow the cliff-like shoreline that leads to the promontory that connects to Chippewa Bay. There I'll stop, unless I see Cassiar Island, and wait for the fog to lift.

No Cassiar, so I shift into neutral and bob in the calm water off the point, killing time in anticipation of the expected clearing. The diesel heater has warmed the boat's cabin nicely, so the wait isn't unpleasant. But it's a lot like waiting for water to boil. I've never been the model of patience.

I tune in the marine forecast on the VHF radio. Most locations are reporting fog or low clouds. Grief Point, the nearest reporting station, has no weather data other than: "Winds calm," one of the few benefits of fog. The south coast forecast calls for a ridge of high pressure to dominate our weather today, with cool, calm conditions that are a setup for prolonged radiation fog. The fog is forecast to dissipate by mid-day, which is right now. But it could be a long wait.

This is similar to many hours spent at small airports, waiting for visibility to increase or the ceiling to lift high enough for takeoff. In such cases, there is often a nearby landmark, maybe a ridge in the foothills, that serves as the reference for a "go" decision. Many times I've waited to see those foothills appear, only to return to a hotel for another night, hoping to see the hills the next day.

Commuting to work on the lake, if you can call it work, requires an appreciation for the power of weather. High winds and their accompanying waves are most dreaded, but low visibility can be a challenge in situations like this. In a comparative way, in my previous

home in Los Angeles, going to work on the infamous freeways have their dangers and their frustrations, to say the very least. Most Californians drive their cars to work solo, but those few who can share a vehicle have the added advantage of car pool lanes. This passenger perk can significantly cut down on commuting time and reduce the frustration factor of heavy traffic. On this lake, there is little traffic, but there are well-traveled commuter lanes, like this one from the promontory at Chippewa Bay to Cassiar Island. Out there on the North Sea, boats could now be crisscrossing, out of sight in the fog.

My commuting lane is closed for now, at least by my self-imposed standards. Then again, it isn't zero-zero here, so I could push out safely into the open water. If I drive slowly, there should be time to see an oncoming boat and get out of the way. That is, of course, if the other boat is also driving slowly. Crew boats know only one cruising velocity – full-speed ahead. Worse yet, a renegade pleasure craft could be pushing its luck with no radar to preclude a collision. Similar to driving the freeways in Los Angeles, no matter how safely you proceed, you could still be in danger. Monitoring your own actions is a lot easier than watching out for the other guy.

After a half-hour of waiting, poking out a ways and coming back, Cassiar Island still doesn't appear. I note the short space on the GPS moving map between here and there. A heading of 160 degrees should take me directly to Cassiar, only a matter of 15 minutes at a fairly slow crawl. Also (I rationalize), as the visibility increases, I'll be able to safely increase my pace.

I check both compasses, which agree with each other within five degrees. This boat is better equipped to make such a blind crossing than the Campion, which ran me in circles on a similarly foggy day (*Farther Up the Lake*, Chapter 14). These compasses combined with my GPS should make the crossing simple. It's not a matter of getting lost. It's a matter of getting hit!

I ease the Bayliner into forward gear and turn the bow to 160 degrees. In idle, I start across, out into the thickest of the fog. Glancing back to see how long it takes to lose sight of land, the shore disappears almost immediately. Yet, there is some forward visibility, which is reassuring. I keep a close eye out for other boats and am prepared to turn around immediately if visibility drops to zero.

I glance down to check my progress on the GPS. When I look back up, the magnetic compass reads "180." In just a matter of seconds, I've gotten off course. Although quickly corrected, it reminds me how fast you can lose your heading in the fog. Flying airplanes under instrument flight rules (IFR) can lead to similar quick excursions in heading and altitude. But I'm more at home in the clouds in an airplane than a boat. And I'm more used to the feel of flight controls.

As the Bayliner crawls across the North Sea, I consider increasing my speed, which will provide less exposure time to any crew boats zipping through this passage. But going faster means reduced closing time with any other vessel, and less opportunity to avoid a collision. It's a tradeoff, like trying to decide whether to run in the rain to avoid getting wet. I elect to crawl and keep a close eye in all directions.

Several times, I catch myself drifting off course to the right, so I make an adjustment by steering an 10 additional degrees to the left for a temporary heading of 150 degrees to get back on course. After a few minutes, I ease back to my computed track of 160 degrees. There's no reason I should miss Cassiar Island on a calm day like today.

There it is – dead ahead, a welcome sight! The island isn't much more than a mound of rocks, and it's right off the bow. The visibility is no worse here than it was on the other side of the North Sea. Neither is it any better.

I ease to the left of the island, avoiding the big rock and the accompanying stumps that stick up near Cassiar's south shore. But there's an unexpected snag sticking up well to the left of the island, and it's completely out of place. I know the rocks and stumps here, and this lump is abrupt and unanticipated. And it's big – it's a boat!

The snag turns into a distinct hull, and I realize how easily the view through the fog can deceive me. I also realize there are other boats out here doing exactly what I'm doing.

I recognize the vessel as Mark's metal boat and small outboard motor, and he's edging his way across my path. We probably saw each other at nearly the same moment. I bet it was an eye-opening surprise for him too.

Mark passes to my right, edging along the shore just as slowly as I am. I blast my horn with two honks as a greeting. Mark, having no horn on his vessel, passes quietly. If I could see anything more than a misty hull in the fog, I'm sure I'd see Mark waving back at me.

Mark eases farther to the right, towards the arm of water that stretches in the direction of Goat Lake. Glimpsing a sign of life in the fog provides me with a sense of relief, but it's a rude reminder that there are other boats plying the same patch of water in these conditions.

From here, I can see the even smaller island that leads to the eastern shore of the lake. This is familiar territory. I push the throttle forward, now traveling at about 10 knots, keeping this well-known shoreline close enough to allow me to identify landmarks in the fog.

I slide past the log boom that sticks out the farthest from shore in this small group of cabins, then along the beach that marks the longest string of land cabins on the lake. At the next promontory, I'll need to ease outward from shore to avoid the grove of stumps that protrude from the far end of the Washout, one of the more dangerous areas of this lake when it comes to prop hazards. But to ease outward, I risk losing sight of the shore in the fog, so I carefully calculate my new heading – call it 170 degrees.

Now I'm out of sight of shore again, but the Washout isn't a large bay, so I'll quickly reach the other side. There I'll find the "palm tree," my personally designated landmark during trips up and down the lake.

It's not a palm, of course. Instead, it's a deformed fir that arcs out over the point like a tropical tree in an advertisement for warmer climates.

I should see the palm tree any moment now. But instead I see a big rock sticking out of the water – straight ahead! Immediately, I shift into reverse, stopping just a few metres from the rock. One both sides of my boat are threatening logs that jut up out of the water. I'm right in the middle of the field of stumps that I've been determined to avoid. Either I drifted to the left or I miscalculated my course. In either case, I need to carefully extract the Bayliner from this hazardous area. I back up a short distance, knowing there are other snags below the waterline that I can't see. Hitting an underwater stump when operating in reverse thrust provides no skeg protection for the prop, so I continue just a few seconds, then shift back into forward gear and slip away into deeper water to the right. It takes only a few minutes, but I hold my breath most of the way.

As soon as I'm comfortably clear of the rock and stumps, I see the palm tree only a short distance ahead. What a comforting sight!

Now I know that I've got it made! I can follow the shoreline all the way around the next big bay, without any further risk of obstacles. In fact, the visibility is now suddenly improved, and I even catch a glimpse of sunlight trying to break through at the point beyond John's cabin. But the reflections on the water are distracting, so I decide to continue to follow the shoreline all the way around the bay rather than cut straight across.

I pass the cabin with the big wall of windows, and there is the campsite on the trail to Inland Lake. I blast the Bayliner's horn to get John's attention: *honk-honk-honk*. Then I break out of the fog into an area of low stratus clouds and good visibility. Passing a short distance off my right side, headed in the opposite direction, is a small boat like mine, reducing speed as it approaches the fog. It's a reminder that the feeling of being alone on this lake today isn't entirely accurate. If our two boats passed in the fog a half-kilometre farther north, we would probably not have even seen each other.

The best sight of the day is John's cabin. He stands on the deck, waving to me, directing me to a parking spot at the edge of the new float foundation. My commute to work is finally complete.

* * * * *

**B**lue barrels are a distinctive component of most float cabins. These air-inflated 55-gallon plastic drums are used to enhance the flotation power of a cedar log foundation, and they've provided to this function on Powell Lake for decades. These drums are sometimes manufactured in other colours, rather than blue. But it's mostly blue barrels that buoy up our float cabins.

You can purchase blue barrels, as John and I did several years ago when we visited a "collector" of these used barrels near Lund. In his back yard, he had stored a pile of barrels. We packed John's truck full of fifteen of them, paying $20 each for these prized possessions. Since then, John hasn't purchased a single plastic drum, although his inventory of blue barrels at all three of his cabins keeps increasing every year. If you keep a close lookout on every trip up and down the lake, your stash of barrels just keeps growing.

Many barrels pop out from under float cabins during storms, drifting to all corners of the lake. If it's near a float cabin, it's appropriate to leave the barrel for the owner to retrieve. But once it drifts well out into the lake, it's fair game. Beachcombers like John will never pass by such a barrel without retrieving it. On most winter days, it would be difficult to travel the length of Powell Lake without encountering at least one free-floating blue barrel.

Today's job in the construction of John's new cabin is to install barrels under the center portion of the float. This is the area where the cabin will be built, and once that construction project is started, getting barrels underneath will be more difficult. Many float cabin owners hire scuba divers to place barrels underneath, but John has been able to install most of his own barrels without going below the water. It takes a bit of maneuvering, and is easiest to accomplish before the float foundation is covered by decking. To prevent the cedar float logs from becoming waterlogged, barrels should be installed during the construction process, although some float cabins begin with only the basic log foundation, later requiring the addition of barrels to raise the waterlogged float. For now, John's new float is riding high, but it will drop lower as the weight of the cabin is added.

We climb up the bridge to shore, then up the cliff to one of the locations where John has stored a mix of nearly new and severely battered plastic drums. Each barrel has two threaded holes on one end, with at least one plastic cap installed. Any crack in the side of a plastic barrel will make it inadequate for flotation, since air will escape over time through even the smallest fracture. Sometimes, it's impossible to find such defects until the barrel is tested with a full load of air.

We haul six barrels down from the storage area. The narrow bridge is a steep descent today, with the lake so low. I walk down to the transition float first, waiting for John to slide the barrels down the bridge. John has positioned two four-by-fours on the edge of the bridge to guide the barrels down. Of course, we could walk the empty barrels down, but that wouldn't be nearly as much fun.

John launches the first barrel, and it slides precisely between the four-by-fours, picking up speed as it descends. Since it's moving faster than I expected, I step out of the way. The barrel slides out onto the transition float, and glides to a stop before reaching the water at the other end.

"Here comes the next one," says John, as he releases another barrel.

The second barrel hangs up when it reaches the bottom, jammed between the lip of the bridge and the edge of the float. I reach over the top of the barrel to tilt it upward and out of the way. Simultaneously, John launches the next barrel before I've cleared the area. Maybe he didn't see that I wasn't finished removing the previous barrel. More likely, he's engaged in a game of human bowling, trying to knock over the pins.

I see the third barrel coming, and have just enough time to step out of the way. But instead, I play John's game – I use the railings on the end of the bridge, like parallel bars, to hop upward as high as I can. The third barrel hits the second and both continue underneath me and out onto the transition float.

"Strike!" I yell. "But you missed the pin boy."

John laughs and slides the next barrel into position. By the time the sixth barrel reaches the bottom of the bridge, I rank his score as two strikes, three spares, and a split. It's impossible to work with John on any project without making it into a game.

✶ ✶ ✶ ✶ ✶

Out on the deck of Cabin Number 1, we prepare the barrels that will go under Cabin Number 5. The 24-by-24-foot center section of the float that will hold the cabin is destined to receive eighteen barrels today, aligned in three rows.

One plastic cap will be installed on each barrel, leaving the other hole open to receive water that we'll use to flood it nearly full. Then we'll slide the neutrally buoyant barrel under and between two adjacent float logs, using a rope to tug it into its assigned position. Once in position, we'll rotate the barrel to assure that the open hole is at the very bottom. Finally, we'll pump compressed air into the hole, which forces the water out. Once the water has been expelled, the barrel remains air tight, with the top hole sealed by the plastic cap and the bottom hole sealed by the pressure of the surrounding water. In this balancing act of air and water, barrels remain fully inflated for many years.

John carefully selects the plastic caps he'll use from a stash he has accumulated. Each must precisely match the threads of the hole, with most barrels having one course-threaded hole and one that's fine-threaded. He selects the best rubber gaskets too, and finishes off the job with Sikaflex waterproof sealant that he disperses from a caulking

gun while I rotate the cap to receive the white pasty substance. John inserts the cap into its hole, and then uses a homebuilt crowbar-like tool for precise tightening. He's careful not to over-torque the cap, which can crack it.

We haul an old air compressor down from the shed. It's an awkward looking contraption that uses an old gasoline engine to power a belt-driven external piston that serves as the compressor. John constructed the apparatus from components he found at an abandoned farm. Using a series of valves and a metal extension wand for the long rubber tubing, we'll be able to pump compressed air into the barrels. John tweaks the compressor on the deck of Cabin Number 1, while sunlight beams down on us. Low scattered clouds that are the remnants of the morning fog are still visible on the distant shore, but it has turned out to be a beautiful afternoon.

\* \* \* \* \*

We use a mix of mostly blue and a few white barrels. Getting the rope into position to pull the drums under the float consumes quite a bit of our time. We devise a system that allows us to pull a new barrel into position and retrieve the rope needed for the next barrel without having to slide the entire rope out from under the float. Only when we change rows do we have to go through the rope rigging process again.

Once the barrel is partially sunk at the edge of the float, we check the cap for leaks. The final test on the cap and the barrel itself will have to remain until it receives its full load of air pressure under the float.

In the first row, we discover a cap that's cracked, and we have to move that barrel back onto the dry deck to replace the cap. On the last row, we find another cap that's not properly sealed. We can reuse the cap, but must once again completely remove the barrel from under the logs to reseal it. In general, the work proceeds well, with our pace increasing as we gain experience with our makeshift process for pulling the barrels into position and filling them with air.

The old compressor takes a lot of babysitting to keep it running. Getting the gas engine started is a tricky process. John pulls the starter rope with one hand and works his other hand over the top of the carburetor, trying to block off the airflow to find the perfect mixture that the engine demands. When it's time to shut down the compressor while we reposition barrels, John uses a crooked stick to flip the spark plug wire loose.

When it comes time to inflate a barrel, I shine a spotlight on the bottom hole, not easy to see two feet below the waterline. John inserts

the metal wand into the hole, sets the compressor valves, and begins to pump air into the barrel. This compressor is an antique piece of machinery, but it does an admirable job for us today.

As the sun drops towards the Bunster Range to the west, we're ready to wrap up our day's work. We feel we've accomplished a lot, regardless of the fog-delayed start. Like most projects with John, I've learned plenty and had lots of fun doing tasks that many would consider mundane. For me, working with a superior aquatic engineer is never tedious or routine. And he bowls a good game.

It's after sunset when I motor northward in the Bayliner, navigating along the commuter lane at high speed. I zoom past the palm tree, the Washout, around Cassiar Island, and through the North Sea. Entering the darkness that now encompasses First Narrows, I can still see sunlight working its way up the nearly vertical face of Goat Island. I cruise by Sandy Beach, past the green navigation light, and into Hole in the Wall. I wiggle my foot inside my boot, and it doesn't hurt even a little bit.

◊ ◊ ◊ ◊ ◊ ◊ ◊

# Chapter 8

# Deck Foundation and Floor Joists

The learning experience from assisting John far overshadows the routine grunt work of construction. But often, simple, focused tasks consume a whole day – reality checks regarding what lies ahead.

Today's task is to set the foundation for the outer deck on each side of the float. This involves moving a split 50-foot log into position on each side of the float foundation, positioning it properly to support the boat docks. John hasn't yet decided whether the outer deck on the north side will be a second low boat dock or merely an extension of the main deck. If a high design is selected, we'll still need the split log on this side as the base for a pony wall. For now, we merely need to lay the foundation for a deck of any height. That foundation, with the flat surface of the split log facing upward, will serve as the starting point for a pony wall (high deck design) or to tie in beams for a lower deck (boat deck design).

When I arrive at the site of Cabin Number 5 at mid-morning, the two segments lie side-by-side on one end of the float. First, we'll need to move one of the split logs from this end of the float and reposition it on the other side. Using peavies to rotate the log and boards as pry bars, we manage to ease the log a few feet to the edge of the float. When we finally push it off into the water, it makes quite a splash!

To maneuver the log to other side of the float requires a lot of joggling. John pushes outward on the breakwater with a pike pole, while I use another pole to guide the log around the outside of the

float and into position to winch up onto the main foundation at the other end of the float.

John hooks up the turfer, using the far end of the brow log as the anchor point. I attach the choker cable onto the end of the split log, and John begins to pump the handle of the winch. The log eases up onto the float.

While John operates the turfer, I make small changes in the path of the split log by using a board to pry between it and the brow log. It's a slow process. Now it's only a matter of easing the split log into an approximate position on this end of the float.

Now we turn our attention to the other half of the log. We mark off its squared position at the edge of the float, where it will span the entire length of the foundation logs. This involves lots of maneuvering with our peavies and pry boards. Along the way, we stop to make measurements of how to best notch and shim the foundation logs to keep the split log level.

Using an axe, John will make notches in the foundation logs, then matching them with cuts on the split log. To do this requires constant rotation of the log to move it off the notching spot. I use a peavy to balance the log on its edge, holding it in a position that allows me to use minimal force – it still takes both hands or sitting on the peavy – while John's notches the logs. Each time we finish a cut, we lay the bubble-level on the flat top of the split log and use a metal square to assure the top is at perfect right-angles to the foundation logs.

Using a level is one way of determining whether our work is acceptable, and then making adjustments as necessary. But water is the best level of all. Along one of the cabin's pony walls, John has laid a green garden hose. When all is level, water added to one end of the hose shouldn't spill out the other end. It's nature's perfect indicator of level conditions on a float cabin.

However, even when you get everything precisely level, don't expect it to last. Add a little weight over here (or walk over there), and everything tilts by the slightest (but measurable) amount. Float cabins can be built level, but they won't stay that way for long unless they are constantly fine-tuned.

As we work, we're entertained by the Comox Coast Guard. Directly across the channel from us, a yellow-and-orange turbine helicopter practices search and rescue operations near a bay surrounded by high

cliffs. We pause in our work to watch the helicopter drop down until it's hovering only a few metres above the surface of the lake. The rotor's downdraft blasts sheets of thick mist high above the helicopter. Then rescue divers jump into the cold March water. The chopper swoops away to the north towards Chippewa Bay, then circles back over us and returns to the drop spot. While the helicopter hovers only 10 metres high, the rescue divers are hauled aboard on cables. They repeat the exercise over and over, concentrated practice for a time when we may need them to save our lives.

"There goes another diver out the door," says John.

That's my cue to grab my pair of pocket binoculars to scan for the latest action. Of course, John sees this with his naked eagle-eyes, but I need my mini-magnifiers to see any of the divers. Even then, they appear as mere red specs in my binoculars.

"I see him," I say. "Look, there's another one."

"Got him," says John (without magnifying lenses, of course).

The helicopter swoops away again, this time south towards the Shinglemill. The chopper circles in that area for a few minutes and then is back on station over its practice area on the opposite shore.

Again and again, the Coast Guard practices their search and rescue techniques. Simultaneously, John and I work at leveling a split log that serves as part of the foundation for the cabin's future deck. For both the Coast Guard and us, the most basic of processes towards our goals take lots of time and repeated attempts.

* * * * *

In contrast to days when headway on the cabin seems barely noticeable are other times when construction seems to progress by leaps and bounds. After plodding forward with the outer deck foundation, our next day of work turns to the floor beams for the cabin itself. John has already constructed the pony walls, so now we need to construct floor joists (beams) that rise from the four-by-four's that form the top of the pony walls.

The 2-inch-by-8-inch boards that John selects for this task are a mix of red cedar for the interior beams and yellow cedar for the more exposed outer structure (since it is even more weather resistant). In a single day, we raise nearly the entire outline of the 24-foot square cabin by eight inches. That's a lot of wood and a highly visible step forward. It makes me feel we are suddenly building a real home.

We work under cloudy skies that occasionally spit out drops of rain. The temperature of about 7 degrees is perfect for a job like this. Even when we must carry long 2-by-8's around the float and perform other heavy tasks, we barely work up a sweat.

* * * * *

As industrious a worker as John might be, he isn't always a model of efficiency. Sometimes I think he purposefully avoids streamlining routine processes. Maybe construction efficiency makes projects seem too much like work. In any case, he occasionally seems to enjoy being purposefully inefficient.

"I need to go get a tape measure," John says, when its time to mark off the cut for the first cabin floor beam with a square.

After returning from Cabin Number 1 with the tape, we continue work on the first joist.

"I'll need a pencil," he now announces.

Off he goes to the cabin again, returning with a pencil. I swear he does this on purpose. For him, half the fun is getting everything set up for each step along the way. Sometimes he'll repeat each extra step methodically, no matter how much wasted motion might be involved.

When we begin to cut the first board, I wonder if we can speed up the measuring process for the lumber that we'll be cutting today.

"All of these boards will be exactly the same length, won't they?" I ask.

"Exactly the same," replies John.

"Would it be good to use this first board as a template for the rest. We could mark off the length on every board we cut, saving us from having to measure each one."

"We could," he says. "But we may as well measure each board. It's almost as easy."

Almost, but not quite. We use the tape measure to mark off each board to exactly the same length, board after board, all day long. John is a master at construction of any type, but he would have problems working in a commercial production line. Which is why he doesn't work in a production line.

The first cabin joists must be aligned carefully. We want the beams to be level, and the footprint of the cabin needs to be square. John uses long screws to join the 2-by-8 cross-beams to the yellow cedar outer

boards. We spend the day measuring lumber, cutting ends with a hand saw, and using a plane to assure all joists meet evenly.

John's work ethics shine through as we shim boards using small strips of tar paper to align joists precisely. There is little doubt that some of the exactness he demands is purely personal. Why we must stop and realign joints between boards isn't always clear to me, but I know it is either because construction sturdiness demands it or John likes it that way. In either case, there is no sense fighting the decision. If John says it has to be exact, it will be exact.

When John takes extra efforts at precise carpentry in areas that will be out of sight, I often toss out one of my favourite sayings: "No one will ever see this."

John's reply is always the same: "But we'll know it's there."

By the time we take our lunch break, we're nearly halfway through the full length of the cabin. Before our eyes today, the cabin is growing upward for the first time in many weeks. Progress!

As we begin to wrap up our work for the day, we take some final measurements. The cabin is destined to sit on a 24-foot square foundation, leaving lots of room for deck on each side. One of our final measurements to confirm that all is well is to extend the measuring

tape from the first joist to the outside side cedar beam (two 12-foot 2-by-8's joined at the middle). I hold one end of the tape measure on the first beam while John carefully straightens out the twisted metal tape.

"It's off," says John.

"What do you mean? How far off?"

"It reads a sixteenth of an inch over 24 feet," he says.

"Sounds good to me," I reply. "So we've got a cabin that's 24 feet and one-sixteenth of an inch long. Surely that's as close as we need to be."

"It's not square," he replies.

"Not square? Are you serious? One-sixteenth of an inch over 24 feet seems plenty satisfactory to me."

"We can fix it," he says. "But it won't be easy."

"What's to fix? Who'll ever know it's not perfectly square?"

"We'll know," says John.

I knew that was coming. It's what I expect from John. And we'd both have it no other way. So we spend an extra hour at the end of our workday fixing it. After all, it's a square cabin.

\* \* \* \* \*

With the floor joists complete, the boards for the floor's base are next. I look forward to this, since it should go fairly fast. And we'll finally have a flat foundation to walk on. Slipping and sliding on wet logs has become a part of the daily routine. To stand on stable, flat boards will be a luxury.

The bottom layer of the floor will consist of planed one-by-eights, with plywood on top. John has chosen this design for both strength and economy. The boards we use aren't a prime cut – low cost but not exact in dimensions. Since these boards will lie under the plywood, they'll need to be matched precisely at their edges.

John uses an electric plane that operates off a gas-driven generator to trim the boards to exact dimensions. The planed boards will form a smooth foundation for the plywood above. Working on the deck of Cabin Number 1, we slide the raw lumber through the planer – a high pitched *rah! rah!* Then each board is hauled to the new float and nailed into place.

In a single day, we lay the boards for half of the floor. The progress shows, as each board is laid in place, squared off at its end, and nailed

into place. We stop after each board to measure the cumulative growth of the floor, careful to adjust gaps between the boards for small variations before they become significant. As we progress, all remains within a sixteenth-inch of error. When we begin to exceed that level of error, we swap boards around to adjust for the inaccuracies. We alternate two 12-foot-long boards with stretches of 16-footers matched with 8-foot lengths. Thus, the boards join at alternating floor joists, improving the overall strength of the floor.

Our first day of floorboard installation is a mix of sun and clouds. Bro lies on the deck in his typical supervisory mode. This is the kind of construction project that suits the black Lab. When a brief sun-shower spits out its big drops, he doesn't budge. When the shower ends, he stands up briefly to shake himself off. Then he resumes his laid-back supervisory pose, watching two workers who have different standards of exactness. But the more precise worker always wins.

◊ ◊ ◊ ◊ ◊ ◊

# Center-of-Book Photos

John and Bro peform quality control

After lockup, with porches added

Kitchen cabinets in-progress

We need more wood!

Hauling in split log with turfer

The 3 steps: Design–Measure–Construct. This is the design process in action.

Using a jack to tighten a cable on the transition float that leads to shore

Deck and docks complete

Number 1 (left), float for Number 5 (center), and Tool Box (right)

# Chapter 9

# Renovating Number 1

In March, John's goals shift. With the floor of Cabin Number 5 contributing a sense of progress, the reality of the costs that lie ahead shift his attention to the renovation of Cabin Number 1. In the long-range plan, Number 5 is a replacement for Number 1, allowing John to sell the older cabin, which will be towed to his southernmost cabin site, Number 4. His cabin numbering system is getting even more complex. Will the moved cabin be called Number 1 or Number 4?

"My cabins aren't numbered," says John. "Only the sites."

"So Number 1 will become Number 4," I reply.

"Sort of."

So what about the Tool Box?

The Tool Box currently sits at site Number 4, and John will tow it north to sit beside Cabin Number 5 as a lockable storage site while finishing the new cabin. But will Cabin Number 5 then be called Cabin Number 1?

One of the first steps in renovating the older cabin involves its float. The foundation is solid, but the float logs ride lower in the water these days, partially waterlogged. The solution is to raise the foundation by installing additional barrels. John purchases twenty at a sale at the local feed and grain store, negotiating a price of $18 per barrel.

The lake's water is too cool this time of year for work without protection, so a professional diver is hired to install the 55-gallon drums. After several delays caused by stormy weather, the twenty barrels finally go under Cabin Number 1. John talks the diver into topping off the air in barrels already under the cabin, and he even convinces him to look for the peavy he lost early in the construction of Cabin Number 5. John directs the diver to the location of the lost implement, and it is found almost immediately.

More importantly (although it's difficult to tell compared to the smile on John's face when the peavy is retrieved), Cabin Number 1 raises four inches, far enough to bring the big foundation logs nicely out of the water again.

There's some minor work needed under the cabin, which John tackles on our first official day of renovation work. Meanwhile, I work with Margy cleaning up the deck boards. The cedar deck is in good shape, but the boards have darkened over the years from persistent assault by the weather and algae. We conquer the slippery slime with algae remover and lots of scrubbing. It takes a full day for Margy and me to complete the deck washing, but it makes the wood look years younger. That night, our backs, shoulders, and upper arms feel the abuse.

A major part of our work involves reducing the clutter in the old cabin. Over the years, a comfortable home can accumulate a lot of excess stuff, and this cabin is no exception. Some of it is better off removed, a good way to make the float cabin look bigger and more presentable for sale.

One day, early in the renovation, John starts hauling old furniture from the deck, dragging it out onto an adjoining raft and then along the boomstick walkway that floats in his back bay. He's headed for the raft, where he'll pile the old furniture that'll be towed back to town and the dump, although some of it includes comfortable treasures that have provided him relaxing days on the porch of Cabin Number 1. Meanwhile, I'm working on a window trim painting project, as assigned. In a nostalgic moment, while lugging a large sofa single-handedly, John stops halfway out the boomstick.

"Hey, Wayne, it's time for a break!" he yells back to me. "Come out and sit here for a few minutes."

The old sofa makes a comfortable place to enjoy a few minutes of relaxation between chores. The April sun beams down on us, as we soak up the glory of the day. Men at work.

Margy is pleased that she can now contribute to the construction of Cabin Number 5, although in an indirect way. It's still too early in the raising of the new cabin for her to feel comfortable working on the new float. Once the decking is installed, she'll feel better about getting around in this demanding work environment. But she can now take a significant part in the renovation of Cabin Number 1.

As the project proceeds, I concentrate on painting assignments. Margy tackles the inside of the cabin, cleaning and reorganizing, starting with the kitchen. She brings the throw rugs outside and scrubs them on the deck, while Bro supervises.

John, Margy, and I (Bro too!) spend several more days cleaning up, tossing out old possessions, and painting doors, trim, and deck furniture. A little effort goes a long ways. This cabin is now fully

presentable and ready to sell. Once John finds a serious buyer, we'll move the cabin south to the Tool Box's current site. Then Number 1 Cabin will become Number 4. John's numbering system demands it.

## Sold!                    * * * * *

It happens faster than expected. Art and Margaret declare their intension to buy the cabin the same day they first see it. They offer a deposit, but John declines: "I trust you," he says.

Trust is one thing, but sometimes John takes things to extremes. On the other hand, the fast sale implies that the cabin is properly valued. If this deal falls through, there will be other customers.

The focus now turns to the site swap between this cabin and the Tool Box at the Number 4 site, five kilometres to the south. We plan to first disconnect the Tool Box and old logs stored next to it, and tow them north, freeing up space for the new cabin. Then we'll tow the cabin down the lake to its new home and cable it to shore.

"Can you meet me at Number 1 tomorrow?" asks John.

"A Saturday? Work on a weekend?"

"You gotta do what you gotta do," replies John.

John reserves his weekends for quad riding and just about anything but work. But the good July weather forecast adds to the temptation to get going with the cabin swap. This is the first full summer that we'll have to work on the new cabin, so we'll need to use this good weather efficiently to get the swap project complete. Then, with that behind us, we'll be able to concentrate on Number 5.

*  *  *  *  *

When I arrive at Number 1, John is hauling hand tools from his shed on shore and loading the tin boat. Bro runs around the dock and up and down the bridge to shore with his normal early-morning enthusiasm.

I help John unload his Hourston, removing his gas-powered grinder, a large jackhammer drill, chainsaw, gas generator, boxes of shackles and cable clamps, piles of rope, and extra cans of gas. We split the load between the small metal boat and my Campion, and then head south to Number 4.

The lake has developed a morning chop that's a challenge for the tin boat, so John eases closer to the shore, where the shadow of the mountains blocks the wind. Bro stands in the bow, sniffing his way down the lake, I cruise in formation farther offshore.

At the Tool Box, we tie up to the half-sinking boat dock that's dangling from the float by a single rope. The end of the dock is underwater, but John makes the slippery leap to the Tool Box, using the semi-submerged dock as a quick step.

"Careful!" he calls back to me. "Real slippery."

If John can make the jump, so can I. I try leaping right at the edge of the dry boarder of the dock, but I miss by a few inches. My left foot pushes off on wet wood and goes out from under me. I come down hard, the inside of my ankle whacking against the edge of the dock. I'll have a hefty bruise tomorrow. Of course, now I'm soaking wet, including my pants and the lower-portion of my T-shirt.

"Told you so," says John? "Are you alright?"

"Hit my ankle hard. But I'll live. At least the water's warm."

When I finally crawl onto the Tool Box's deck, I remove my small author's notebook from my pocket and spread it out to dry on the deck. I pull off my watch and place it beside the notebook. I could fall again, but there will be nothing else to harm by getting wet.

I carefully step back down to the mostly-submerged boat dock, this time stepping in a foot of water and not worrying about it. I edge my way back to the tin boat with John (who again jumps over the wet area), and we bring the rest of the load onto the deck. I carry the big grinder, which hampers my balance a bit. When I step into the slippery section of the dock that leads to the Tool Box, my feet go out from under me again. When I slam down again, I manage to hold the heavy grinder high and out of the water.

"Watch the grinder!" I yell to John.

Tool abuse is a sin. I'm sure that John is more concerned with his grinder than me.

"It's okay John. I'm not injured."

"Thanks for protecting the grinder," says John, as I pull myself out of the water.

We both get a good laugh over my second spill, as I swing the grinder onto the float, and then pull myself up.

"Careful where you walk," says John. "These boards are toast."

It's a good description of the situation. The old cedar boards are so fragile that they break like toast if you step on them in the wrong place. Several of the planks have already been broken, hanging down at odd angles, with a view straight to the water below. Walking over the lines of nails, directly over the beams, solves the problem. But later this morning, I step slightly off the nail line, and my already injured ankle gets another whack when I crash through the decking.

After we reorganize our tools, we take the tin boat to shore to establish four anchor points on the surrounding rock cliffs to hold the cabin. The Tool Box has been secured by only one cable and three ropes. This has been adequate for a small float, but the cabin will need cables that are properly placed.

John selects a symmetry that will require two long cables stretched nearly the full length of the small bay, along with two shorter cables that run inward nearly directly to shore. The long cables will force the cabin outward, and the shorter cables will try to keep the cabin in towards shore. It's a balancing act that minimizes stress on the cables, and a game that John knows well.

We perch ourselves on the rock ledge, while John sets up the jackhammer drill he has borrowed from a friend at the paper mill. A 1-inch bit is installed, while the gas generator remains in the tin boat to power it. He starts the generator and begins to drill.

It's a noisy process, but I'm surprised how quickly the drill grinds into the granite. A gray powder builds around the bit, higher and higher, as the drill pulverizes the rock. In just a few minutes, John has drilled 8 inches into the solid cliff.

Then we pound a steel rod into the hole, using a sledgehammer, first bending the rod slightly to ensure a solid fit. Using the gas-powered grinder, John cuts off the excess rod, and then adds two heavy links of chain to hold the cable, topping it off with a cable clamp to prevent the chain from coming off.

We go through the shoreline drilling process four times, completing the anchor pattern for the new cabin. We'll leave the cable attachments until we bring the cabin to the site. For now, we rope the Tool Box to the new anchor rods to test the geometry, using shackles to attach the ropes. This way, we'll be able to quickly detach the ropes even when

Cable Clamps    Shackle

they're stretched under load, making the cabin swap faster and more efficient.

Site Number 4 contains old cedar and fir logs of various sizes, floating and tied to the booms and the Tool Box. Like all of John's float cabin sites, a good log is never thrown away. Someday it may be needed for a raft, breakwater, or some other purpose. So we'll need to move these logs with the Tool Box.

John rounds up the logs with his pike pole while I tie them to the float, arranging them in a streamlined fashioned on both sides and at the rear of the Tool Box. One of the lake's smallest floats is gradually growing, and we'll tow the whole assembly north.

At the end of the day, we take the tin boat back to shore and hike up the cliff to the smooth high-ground that looks down to the small bay. Through the trees, it's a scenic view.

We continue farther uphill, crossing a small creek that runs year-round. John has used a black garden hose to harness this water, for no real reason, during his visits to the Tool Box. The new owners will inherit a rare location where fresh water can be brought down from

this spring-fed creek using the most efficient pumping system in the universe – gravity.

"I'm gonna have a hard time giving up this spot," says John.

I can see it in his eyes. The Tool Box has been just a placeholder among float cabin sites, but he has always loved this place.

* * * * *

We meet at Number 4 the next morning at 7 o'clock. It'll be necessary to get an early start to beat the up-lake winds that develop nearly every morning during the summer. For towing, a smooth lake is vastly preferred.

We unhook the shackles that hold the Tool Box to shore and attach a tow rope to my Campion. John circles around the small bay in his Hourston, supervising the tow, while I have the honour of pulling the Tool Box out of its spot. John unhooks the breakwater (also temporarily attached by rope and shackle the previous day), using the Hourston to pull the line of logs away from shore.

"Go for it!" he yells to me.

I shift into gear and start slowly forward. The tow rope grabs, and the Tool Box begins to swing outward from shore, along with its accompanying logs, a floating walkway, and a huge decorative stump. We're underway!

I angle north, starting up the lake, while John remains behind, securing the breakwater behind us. When I glance back, it's a strange site. Seeing the Tool Box in this small cove every time I drive up the lake, it's now an empty bay, looking bigger and more scenic than ever.

I settle into a slow tow at 1200 RPM, providing about 3 knots of forward progress. This will result in a tow-time of a little over an hour in the glassy morning water.

In our last-minute arrangements at the Tool Box this morning, Bro ended up in my boat, curled up and nearly asleep as John and I disconnected the ropes. When we begin the tow, he's still in the Campion, and now stuck in the boat with me for the slow tow to the north. At first, he's comfortable with this, since slow boats are his favourite. But now he sits up and sees John zipping around us in the Hourston. Away from his master, Bro is fidgety. When John slips past

us in the Hourston, headed to Number 1 to prepare the breakwater for our arrival, Bro goes into a frenzied pant, forelegs propped up on the brow cushions. He remains in the bow, next to a pike pole, engaged in a nervous pant for the entire trip.

I throw out a trolling line, with a red-and-white daredevil attached. It's the perfect speed for trolling, so why waste the opportunity? My lure rides far behind the Campion, probably under and behind the Tool Box.

When John returns in the Hourston, he rides in formation with me for a while, and Bro barks an enthusiastic welcome. John pulls up behind the Campion and ties up to the stern. His boat rides in-tow behind us, with the Tool Box and its entourage of logs following behind. John climbs onto the Campion's swim grid and into my boat. Bro is elated to be reunited with his master again, and rubs against everything in sight, especially John.

As we approach Number 1, John hops back aboard his Hourston. Bro will have to remain in the Campion a while longer, since it's not an easy leap to the other boat.

John slips away, now dropping behind the Tool Box to be prepared to push it into position against the outside of the breakwater. We have decided to tie up first to the breakwater, untie the trailing logs, and bring things into the breakwater in sections.

I ease off on the throttle, slowing and finally shifting into neutral to let the Tool Box drift and finally settle near the breakwater. John uses the Hourston to push it into position against the boom.

We disconnect the logs from the Tool Box, and John pushes them into the breakwater entrance. He returns for the walkway and stump, and finally joggles the Tool Box through the entrance, into its temporary position next to the new float cabin we're building. The small bay is now very full – the original cabin, the new cabin's float, the Tool Box, and miscellaneous wood.

The first part of the cabin swap is complete.

◊ ◊ ◊ ◊ ◊ ◊ ◊

# Chapter 10

# Cabin Swap

No sooner is the Tool Box floating in its new home at Site Number 1 than the visitors arrive. When something changes on the lake, such as the appearance of a cabin at a new spot, everyone wants to know the details.

Jess is first to arrive. He motors into the narrow entrance at Number 1, his skookum barge-boat pushed by a 50-horse outboard.

"What's goin' on?" says Jess.

"Just brought this one in," replies John, gesturing towards the Tool Box. "Sold my cabin, and they get the spot on the south end of the lake."

The big just-sold cabin is now packed in even tighter among the plethora of floating logs, rafts, docks, a new float under construction, and now the Tool Box. This site is plenty full.

The metal barge bobs next to the Tool Box, while John and I take a break from our task of securing logs. Jess's young son fishes off the deck of the big boat, throwing what looks like a naked sinker as far as he can. Jess stays in the boat, supervising.

"Rock bottom!" calls out the young lad after each cast settles.

It seems like an astute statement from a child so young. Jess laughs, like it's something he's used to.

"Might catch a bullhead," says John.

"Doubt it," replies Jess. "No hook on the line. Just a sinker – it's a lot safer."

And good practice for the real thing someday. While we talk, the little boy casts and retrieves his sinker faithfully, reeling in time after time: "Rock bottom!" he keeps calling out.

John and I sit on the edge of the Tool Box deck, feet dangling down to the cedar log foundation. Jess and John swap fish stories, while I listen.

"Went to Goat Lake yesterday," says Jess. "On the way back we trolled most of the way. Caught a bunch of two and three pounders."

I remember Jess telling me this tale about his fishing trip a few days ago. But that story involved one and two pounders. In tales of fishing, each episode must grow over time, especially specific numbers and weights.

When Jess and his son motor out of the breakwater entrance, another small boat is headed around the point and towards us.

"That's Bert," says John. "He saw us towing past his cabin, and now he wants to know what's goin' on."

Bert pulls up towards the Tool Box in his tin boat, cuts his outboard, and drifts the remaining few feet. I help him tie up. Like Jess, he stays in his boat while he talks.

"New cabin?" says Bert, motioning to the Tool Box.

"Just my lower-lake shed," says John. "Movin' it up here to make room for my other cabin."

"Sold it?" asks Bert.

"Not quite yet," replies John. "But I've accepted an offer."

"Well, I just came over to see if I could borrow a phone. Need to make a rather critical call, and my battery is dead."

"You can use mine," I intervene. "Let me get if for you from my boat."

When I return with the phone, I hand it to Bert: "Be sure to dial one and 604 first, even though it's just local."

"I'm only calling town. Be just a minute."

Bert makes the phone call from his boat, while John and I sit on the edge of the Tool Box. A little privacy is only fair, but it's tough to get in a boat tied up only a few feet away.

"Hey, this is Bert," he says into the phone. "I've been trying to call Mom, but she isn't answering her phone. Can you give her a message?"

Calling your mom could be critical. Or at least important.

"Let her know we need some things when she comes up the lake," says Bert. "Pop of any kind and some toilet paper."

Bert hangs up soon after delivering the brief message, and hands the phone back to me.

"Thanks," he says. "Gotta go now. Good luck with the sale of the cabin."

With that, Bert makes a single pull on the starter rope, and the engine catches immediately. He promptly motors out of the breakwater entrance and is up on plane almost immediately, on his way back to his cabin.

"Didn't sound like a very important telephone call to me, " says John. "Everybody's just got to see what's goin' on."

* * * * *

John and I spend the rest of the day preparing Cabin Number 1 for its move south. We disconnect the cables to shore, replacing them with ropes on shackles that will be easily removed on the day of the move. Since the new float is roped to the old cabin, we need to secure it to shore with new cables.

We use lots of rope and a seemingly endless number of clamps and shackles for temporary connections, walking logs back and forth between the new float and shore, or sometimes we use the tin boat. When connecting new cables, we ride on the firewood raft, pulling ourselves along by rope or pushing with a pike pole.

The sequence of events keeps repeating itself, since John has a structured scatter-work sequence that I've learned to understand over the years. He refuses to act too organized during repetitive tasks, probably since it would be boring that way. He seems intent on making extra work for himself at times, just letting things happen. Since one of my most important tasks is to hand John tools and hardware – an assignment I take seriously and that I know he appreciates – I sometimes find the unstructured process a bit frustrating.

"Hey, Wayne, could you bring me a shackle? One of the small ones in the bag over there."

"Sure, John," I say, as I clamber over a pile of firewood in the middle of the dock, then around the gas generator covered by a tarp.

When I finally make it to the shackles, I yell back: "Shall I just bring the bag?"

"No, we don't need it."

I climb over the obstacles, back to where John is waiting for me so he can complete the task.

"Looks like I'll need a crescent wrench," says John, as I hand him the shackle.

"Where?"

"Back there by the bag of shackles."

I hop over the firewood pile and around the generator again. When I return with the wrench, John announces the next step.

"Well, we're just about ready to hook onto the cable with the turfer. I think I left the handle in the boat."

So off I go to the Hourston, stepping from one floating log to another. I wouldn't be surprised if he sends me back to the boat for a hammer next.

"Now I'll need to attach a cable clamp so we can hook on with the turfer."

And where are the cable clamps? Answer: in the bag with the shackles! This time, in defiance of John, I return with the whole bag.

\* \* \* \* \*

**P**reparation of the breakwater entrance is one of today's biggest challenges. Here, too, the cable clamps are removed and a rope installed as a replacement for the normal steel cable. But our decision to make the disconnection at the shore anchor point on the cliff means we must pull the cable onto the breakwater so we don't lose the shore end. Long cables are heavy, and pulling one out of deep water can be a nearly-impossible process.

Using John's tin boat, we zip back and forth to shore. Without it (or a raft), the process would be even more difficult. But in a single afternoon, we progress faster than expected. Tomorrow morning we'll be ready to move the cabin to its new spot at old Number 4.

\* \* \* \* \*

**J**ust before 7 o'clock in the morning, I arrive at Cabin Number 1, with Margy as my passenger in the Campion, both of us looking forward to the big event. We hover outside the breakwater, while I cast against the logs for trout. The mountains to the east still shade this spot from the morning sun, and will do so for another three hours, even during

July. Conditions are perfect for the move – not a hint of the typical up-lake summer winds yet.

After I've completed a few casts, John pulls up in his Hourston, with his mother and father as passengers. Bro is also there, of course, pushing his hose over the gunnel, barking a "Good morning!"

"Look who I've got," says John. "Dad has never missed a move of one of my cabins."

The process of disconnecting the ropes that temporarily secure the cabin to shore is fast. With the shackles installed yesterday, all is ready in less than a half hour. We'll use my boat for the tow, since the engine is more powerful, so I hook up the tow line, while John uses his tin boat to go to shore at the connection point for the breakwater. After unhooking the rope at the quick-disconnect shackle, he begins to push on the breakwater with the bow of the tin boat, easing it outward.

"Let's get going!" yells John back to me in the Campion. "You can help me push the breakwater open with your boat."

Margy, Ed, and Helen are standing under the cabin's front porch, and John's Hourston is tied to the rear of the float, as is the firewood raft that will be needed for work later at Number 4. We're ready to go!

I ease forward in the Campion, while Ed assures the tow line stays clear of my prop. Before the rope is at it's full 50-foot length, the bow of the Campion is up against the breakwater, working with John's tin boat to push the opening wide enough for the cabin to pass through. It's a slow, gentle process that presses outward at a constant pace.

"You're clear," yells John, when he sees there's enough space for the cabin to get out.

I angle slightly to the left, and the cabin starts to follow me. The tow line is tight now, and the cabin swings to align with my boat. We're under way!

Behind me, I watch John zipping around in his tin boat, checking the clearance with the breakwater (tight but adequate), then hurrying to the rear of the cabin to make sure the breakwater doesn't close on its own momentum too soon.

A passing boat, headed north, slows briefly to watch the event, then continues on. Another smaller boat stops, while the woman in the bow snaps photos.

"That's the new owners!" John yells over to me.

Their boat drifts closer to my Campion, but safely out of the way of the passing float cabin.

"Must be an exciting day for you!" I yell across to the new owners, Art and Margaret.

"Really exciting!" yells Margaret. "We can't wait to get into the cabin."

"I'm Wayne!" I yell back. "That's my wife, Margy, on the cabin deck, along with John's mom and dad."

I'm not sure that Margaret and Art hear any of my explanation, especially now that I've increased power to 1200 RPM. In a few minutes, after photos from a variety of camera angles, they head south, probably down to Number 4 or maybe back to town. John has told me that he called the new owners last night to tell them about the move. They didn't think they would be able to be present because of commitments in town this morning. But they obviously stole a few moments from wherever they were supposed to be to see the big event. I hope they'll be nearly as happy as I've been with float cabin life.

Within a few minutes, I'm out of the shoreline shadows and into the open water where the sun is shining. I gradually ease south towards Number 4. John slips farther behind, securing the breakwater behind us. The cabin tows straight and easy.

Within the first few kilometres, John is back, riding formation behind me. He eases in even closer, and throws me a rope. I tie it to the cleat on the side of the Campion's stern, leaving plenty of slack to allow the tin boat to ride well clear of my boat. Then I pull on the rope to drag John's boat close enough for him to come aboard.

John climbs out onto the bow brace of the tin boat and jumps onto the Campion's swim grid. Once aboard, I play out the tin boat's bow rope to its full length.

John now drives, while I try some more trolling. Art and Margaret are back again now, circling us and the cabin in wide arcs. Then they come back up and ride formation with the Campion, just off our left side. John talks to them briefly, and away they go again – this time to finally meet their scheduled obligations in town. A few minutes late because of an event this important should be a tiny thread in the fabric of life.

When we are within a few kilometres of Number 4, John climbs back into the tin boat, and I disconnect his bow line. He peels off and

turns back to the towed cabin to work on some rope connections that will be needed at the new spot. I watch Ed and him working on one side of the cabin, while Margy and Helen sit on a bench on the other side. It looks like business as usual on a float cabin, but it's traveling down the lake at 3 knots. Moving day!

John departs the cabin in the tin boat again, rushing ahead of me to open the breakwater for our arrival. In the morning shadows, I'm not entirely certain where Number 4 lies, although I pass it on each trip up and down the lake. This morning, everything is in shadows, and all the indentations in the shoreline look alike. It's no big deal, since I'll recognize the spot before I pass it. But if I see it too late, it'll be an awkward turn at the last minute. When John's boat pops into the sunshine briefly as he maneuvers along the breakwater at Number 4, I'm grateful for a clear marker.

I watch John work on the boom. He seems to be experiencing some difficulties, but there's no task too big for John. He opens the spot perfectly in advance of our arrival, I come back on the throttle a bit, and the cabin slips slowly towards shore.

Although I'm concerned about properly sliding the cabin into the spot, all goes nearly flawlessly. When I approach the shoreline, I slow to idle well in advance of our arrival, giving the cabin plenty of time

to catch up with my boat. I judge the swing almost perfectly, and the cabin glides neatly into place. John maneuvers between the cabin and shore to assure I haven't cut it too close, and I haven't. When we're clear of all obstacles, he swings alongside the cabin and begins pushing the float into its final position with the tin boat. This is my cue to coast and shift into neutral. A few minutes later, Ed signals to me to unhook the tow line. The cabin is no longer in my control.

It only takes a few minutes to hook up the lines to shore, using the shackled ropes we left in position the day before. One of the cliff anchor points isn't the seemingly-perfect geometry we calculated the day before with the smaller Tool Box. Ed recommends that we abandon one of our drilled locations and establish a new connection around a stump. This gives the inward pull on the cabin a heftier angle to work with, and it's simple to adapt to the revised plan.

Once the four cabin-to-shore ropes are secure, the cabin settles into its new spot perfectly. When the wind catches us, nothing moves. When we replace the ropes with cables, this spot will be even more secure. Moving day is successfully complete.

When Margy and I and motor out for our trip home, John and his parents (Bro too!) are still aboard the float. We stop outside the breakwater for a photo of the cabin in its new location. It looks terrific

in this spot, sure to provide the new owners with decades of glorious float cabin experiences.

*****

The next morning is a leisurely 9 o'clock departure from Hole in the Wall. I could leave even later, but I'll need to tow the firewood raft from the new cabin location at Number 4 to Mowat Bay to meet John. That should take about 45 minutes. At Mowat, John will meet me with spools of heavy steel cable in the bed of his truck, needed to secure the cabin permanently at Number 4.

When I arrive at Number 4, the raft is tied to a stump, with a short tow rope on the other end. I unhook the raft from the stump, and maneuver out of the narrow breakwater entrance. It's a bit tight, but I joggle the raft against the inside of the boom until it floats free. Once outside the breakwater, I add another 50 feet of rope to the tow line and angle south towards Mowat Bay.

With the streamlined flow of the raft, I can push the throttle up to 1400 RPM, providing nearly 5 knots in already choppy water. The raft follows nicely, and it's an easy 30 minutes to Mowat.

As I approach the dock, I can see John's truck parked on one of the two launch ramps. Looking closely, I notice two wooden spools of cable in the pickup bed. John paces the dock, while Bro scouts along the shoreline, looking for critters.

I swing to the left before docking, allowing the raft to drift close enough for John to grab. By the time I maneuver into the open area at the other launch ramp, John is there to help me with docking. He has already tied up the raft, so we'll only need to move it shoreward slightly to align with the tailgate of his truck.

Loading the heavy spools of cable is relatively easy, since the tailgate of the truck is nearly the same height as the raft's brow log. We tug and push the spools until they're securely in place on the raft. One of the wooden spools is so rotted that pieces come apart in our hands. But the cable, although rusted, looks sturdy and without frays.

Just as we finish loading, Fritz arrives in his small sailboat. John walks out to meet him, since the natural place for him to tie up is on the raft side of the dock, but we want open space to maneuver when we leave. My boat is blocking the other side, so John helps Fritz move his sailboat around the Campion. Now I'll be able to pull in next to the raft to tie to it when we're ready to go.

All in all, everything works smoothly, and I'm away from the dock in just a few more minutes. John will drive his truck from here to the Shinglemill, and then take his boat to Site Number 1 (which is now the location of Number 4's Tool Box and the new float that will become Cabin Number 5 – the numbers are becoming complicated). There he'll retrieve his tin boat and bring it back to Site Number 4. The small boat will come in handy during the cable installation we have planned for today. When moving stuff around on the lake, nothing is simple. Today it will take three boats and a raft, plus John's pickup truck, of course.

When he catches up to me in his Hourston, I'm halfway to Number 4. He rides in formation with me for a few minutes while we discuss our plan of attack.

"Maybe we can get by without the tin boat," says John. "We can operate off the raft, and save a trip up to Number 1."

Good idea. This will reduce the number of boats to two. But we should have thought of it beforehand. That would have allowed us to use only my boat today, rather than both the Campion and Hourston.

John continues riding formation, since there is now no need for him to go to Number 1, but we drift far enough apart so we can't talk

over the sound of our engines. Riding closer together takes too much continuous attention.

I cast out my trout lure, a red-and-white daredevil, and begin trolling. It's probably a bit to fast for profitable trolling, since the raft is being towed at considerable speed. But my fishing pole bends back as if it's ready to catch a big one. Most likely, my lure is cruising underneath the raft, which may be a good place to catch a fish. (But I don't.)

When we arrive at Number 4, it's an easy entry through the breakwater with John's help guiding the raft with the pushing force of his bow. He positions the raft up against the cabin, and we take a break for lunch.

John surveys the site once again, trying to decide how to most easily install the cables. He stands on the raft, pondering the situation, looking for the most efficient way to attack the task.

First we must make a loop in each of the four cables at the cabin end. The two longest cables are still on the spools. For the two shorter cables that will connect nearly directly to shore, John has already cut the segments to size at home. Since the cabin is already properly placed, we only need to tie off the loops at the cabin end with a pair of cable clamps, and then pull the cables to shore for the second loop and the second set of clamps.

"Never saddle a dead horse," I say, as John contemplates a tricky cable connection. "I remember the first time you taught me that."

It's a good way to remember how to install the cable clamp on the loop. The tail (dead end) gets the U-shaped bracket of the cable clamp, assuring maximum holding power. Each loop gets two clamps, with the bolts tightened to John's industrial-strength torque standards.

Long cables are heavy, but we use the raft to assist as a transport platform. We pull ourselves to and from shore using the ropes we installed yesterday.

The longer cables take a lot more grunt work, as does the breakwater cable that was replaced with a rope so the entrance could be easily opened and closed off during the move. But in only a few hours we're done. Cabin Number 1 (now at Site Number 4 – this will forever mess up the numbering system) is ready for the new owners!

I'm surprised at our efficiency today. We've made lots of progress in less time than anticipated. We still have a few hours before supper, so we decide to use it to finish the breakwater repairs at Site Number 1 (where Cabin Number 1 was removed yesterday, now the site of Cabin Number 5!). John goes north in his Hourston to prepare the breakwater for work. Meanwhile, I hook up to the raft again, and start to tow it north. The raft has proven to be a fine work platform for cable, and we'll be able to use it again on this final task of the day.

We find the breakwater entrance cable at Cabin Number 5 to be the hardest job of all. It is a long cable that has to be pulled all the way to shore. In the process, the cable gets hung up on an underwater snag or rock, and we have to start the process all over. But we push and pull and finally overcome ever-powerful gravity. It's a tough fight, but our last one today. Done! And home in time for supper.

◊ ◊ ◊ ◊ ◊ ◊ ◊

# Chapter 11

# Anchor Drop

John now turns his attention to the boom that protects his cabin site. The lower lake is wide open to the south, and storms traditionally move in from the southeast, up the lake. Additionally, outflow winds can cause havoc when northwest winds drop down out of Chippewa Bay – what John calls CB-CB'ers, Chippewa Bay Cabin Busters (Up the Lake, Chapter 7).

The original breakwater at Cabin Number 5 (when it housed Cabin Number 1) was a hearty multi-rowed wall of logs, dragging the original boom anchor inward over time. Now the clearance between the breakwater and the new float is so close that west winds push the logs nearly to the cabin foundation, temporarily closing off the water route to the north end of his protected area. A new anchor is needed, and additional logs would enhance the overall protection of the cabin site. John decides to tackle both projects before proceeding with any further cabin construction.

**\* \* \* \* \***

When I arrive at the Cabin Number 5 work site, John's dad, Ed, is paddling a big raft with a shovel, while John yells instructions from the tin boat that floats nearby. Both are in the inside-the-boom area to the north of the float, and it looks like Ed is headed out the breakwater entrance.

I come off-plane in the Campion and drift to a stop a few feet outside the breakwater, shut off the engine, and step to the back deck to try to figure out what's going on.

"Where you going, Ed?" I yell across the ten metres separating me from him.

He glances up, but says nothing, as if it's perfectly normal to be paddling a big raft containing a mound of sand, two big blue barrels, and a huge pile of rope – with a shovel. Behind the blue barrels, I can see an elaborate structure of heavy chains and intricately-knotted heavy rope.

"Hey, Wayne!" yells John. "Just in time to see the drop."

That's why I'm here. And I knew John and Ed were building a contraption to drop the new anchors from the raft. But I hadn't pictured it quite this way.

The sand is left over from the mix of cement for the barrels. The release device is typical of Ed – a distinct configuration of precisely

levered ropes to keep the heavy barrels on the edge of the raft, balanced until the proper moment of release outside the breakwater.

Bro is aboard the tin boat with John, which pulls up behind the raft and gives it a hefty push. It would be a long way paddling with a shovel.

"You're late," says John.

"Not that I know," I reply. "I thought you said 10 o'clock."

"Almost missed it. It's nearly 11 o'clock."

"Not in my time zone," I answer. "This is standard time these days, you know."

"No, I didn't notice," says John.

Which figures. I changed my clock when daylight savings time ended three days ago. John will change his when he gets around to it.

"You're in your own time warp," I yell across the breakwater. "And no phone either."

The local telephone company has been in and out of service for several days, a victim of a fire at a major switching station. So I haven't talked to John since the time change, but I knew he planned to get going with the anchor drop today at 10 o'clock. Of course, that's in his time zone.

Recently, in a CB-CB'er, John's breakwater boom smashed against the new float at Number 5, knocking a pony wall (still under construction) loose. Additionally, the storm destroyed his temporary boat dock, irregular boards nailed to the float structure.

The old barely-floating (and motorless) boat that rides behind the float was also damaged when the storage dock for the tin boat whacked into its hull below the water line. None of the damage was severe, considering the temporary state of everything at Number 5. Even the damage to the old boat isn't worth worrying about – just another source of leakage in an already leaky structure. We'll need to beach it soon to fix the leaks and take care of the multitude of repairs that will eventually be needed if John keeps this hulk much longer. It was originally intended as a quad hauling barge, but now it sits behind the float holding old lawn chairs and discarded items that can safely sit in two feet of stagnant water.

The storm was a wakeup call to a job that John has put off for some time, dropping a new anchor farther out to reposition his boom properly. And while work stoppage on the cabin is leading to frustration, it's something constructive to do in the meantime.

With the raft positioned near the drop point, Ed takes charge of the pending drop operation while John uses the tin boat to verify the proper spot for the new anchor. He drives back and forth in front of the breakwater, checking line-of-sight to shore, triangulating the position for the drop. Then he uses the tin boat to nudge the raft to the north by a few metres, and then backs away.

"Let 'er go when you're ready!" John yells to Ed. "Make sure your feet aren't tangled in the rope."

Ed nods. There's no doubt he has already taken special caution to keep clear of the dropping rope. But he doesn't look comfortable on the raft, which is leaning precariously to the side with the cement-filled barrels. He stands a few feet back from the ropes, with his shoes a half-foot underwater.

I hover well clear of the raft, while John tucks in fairly close on the north end. Ed carefully disconnects the master knot that holds the barrels securely to the raft. Then, with no more than a gentle (and careful) kick of one of the barrels, the two heavy anchors tip towards the water, teeter for a moment, then fall towards the lake surface.

It's a simultaneous *Splash!* and *Thunk!* as the big plastic barrels full of concrete hit the water. The thick rope whirls as it unwinds from its purposeful stack. Then it's quickly all over. The new anchors are down, while a boat fender floats at the scene, marking the end of the rope.

John swoops over to grab the end the fender, and ties the rope securely to a ring in the boom. He gives a thumbs up to Ed, then he comes back to push him and the raft back through the boom entrance. Ed now stands on an untilted raft, shaking one wet foot then the other, despairingly. But at least no more shoveling is required.

# Chapter 12

# Haulin' Lumber

During the bout of winter storms that delays any outside work, John has done his best to fill the intervening period with little projects on the cabin, including tasks involving cleanup – reorganizing piles of lumber, adding wood screws where we initially set the position of boards with a single nail, and a multitude of minor jobs. As essential as these tasks might be, the cabin visually shows little progress as I pass it during my winter trips up and down the lake.

We're now into the venture's second spring, totaling 20 months since the first float log slid into position. By May, we're well underway again. John has found a respectable bargain on bulk lumber, and we need to move it from town to the cabin. For this purpose he develops a temporary redesign of a boat trailer to handle the task. The newly-purchased boards go directly from the lumber yard onto the trailer, then to Powell Lake. With the boards bundled together tightly, the load is launched from the trailer into the water at Mowat Bay, a large barely-floating stack to be towed to Number 5.

John makes a test run of the hauling procedure while I'm in the States, and he's ready for another load when I return in early June. After getting settled in my cabin I motor down the lake on a sunny morning to meet John at Mowat Bay.

The dock at Mowat is small but efficient. A launch ramp on each side enhances operations, and we won't be holding up boat traffic so early in the morning. But when I arrive, Fritz's red sailboat, with his big sail fully deployed is parked on the side of the dock that I had planned to use. Fritz's sail flops loosely in the breeze, he loads goods purchased in town, getting ready to return to his all-season home in Three-Mile Bay. My only alternative is to park on the other side of the dock.

"Hi, Fritz!" I yell, as I hop out of the Campion.

I'm about 10 metres away, and the engine on my boat is still idling, so I don't fully comprehend Fritz's reply. But it has something to do with North Korea. Fritz is forever cognizant of geopolitical issues, and I'm not sure how to avoid a discussion when I know that John will want to get going quickly.

"I've heard a little about the Korean situation, but I haven't been following it very closely. Nice seeing you Fritz!"

And it is. Fritz is the only other full-time resident of Powell Lake, and I respect him. In all seasons, Three-Mile Bay is alive with human activity, similar to our cabin in Hole in the Wall. When people kiddingly compare me to Fritz, I'm flattered.

John has just pulled in with his truck. He comes out onto the ramp, yelling a "Hello!" to Fritz, and stopping briefly to talk to him.

"I'd rather use the other side of the dock," John says. "But Fritz's boat is in the way."

"No problem. We can offer to help him move it."

Sure enough, Fritz is glad to move his sailboat so I can maneuver around to the other side of the dock. As his boat swings awkwardly with the sail fully unfurled in the breeze, the three of us reposition it at the end of the dock. Then Fritz and I have an abridged discussion about North Korea and Iranian military buildups. I don't always understand his animated points of discussion, but I respect what he has to say.

I move the Campion to the other side of the dock, my stern in position for an easy hookup to the stack of lumber. Meanwhile, John backs the trailer down the ramp. Once deep enough in the water, he walks back to the trailer, and pushes the load off with a single swift kick with one leg. The bundled boards bob gently behind the trailer.

"Ready to go," he says, as he walks down the dock with the tow line, hooking it to the stern of the Campion. "Go slow, or the load will want to flip over."

"Okay. I'll keep it below 50 miles per hour. See you at Number 5."

I start the motor, while John unhooks my docking lines. I pull slowly forward, easing clear of Fritz's sailboat. As I look back, I see the tow rope straightening. Bro and John stand on the dock, watching me take up the slack.

When I'm well clear of the dock, I return the throttle to neutral as the load pulls tight against the rope. Then I shift into forward again, and begin to tow. In just a few minutes, I'm able to increase the RPM to 1400, moving nicely at about 5 miles per hour. The load tows crooked, but it remains right side up.

In another 30 minutes, I'm halfway to Cabin Number 5, and John has already caught up with me. In this short time, he has returned the trailer to the airport hangar, driven to the Shinglemill, and boarded his boat for the trip up the lake. He now pulls up behind me in his Hourston to inspect the load close-up. Then he maneuvers forward and next to me, giving me a thumbs-up.

John zooms ahead to Number 5, while I settle back and enjoy the tow. My boat's radio is tuned to CBC, and I listen to a debate about the upcoming winter Olympics. There's little doubt this will be a historic event for British Columbia, but the naysayers are concerned with the costs of security and the impact on the homeless. It's a typical battle between good and evil, but it's not entirely clear which is which.

When I arrive at Number 5, John is ready for me, floating near the breakwater in his tin boat. When he pulls up next to me, I throttle back to idle.

"Want me to tow it in?" he asks.

"Sure. That will save us some time, knowing me and towed objects."

So John takes over with his tin boat, shortening the rope, and maneuvering the load through the breakwater entrance with a single arcing swoop that doesn't miss a beat. In just a few minutes, the bobbing stack of lumber is tied to the float foundation. After another half hour of labour, all of the boards are stacked in neat piles on the deck.

I love the sight of stacked lumber at Number 5. It means substantial progress is about to occur. And I'll notice the results each time I cruise up and down the lake.

\* \* \* \* \*

The early part of summer (the second for this cabin project) is spent on deck construction, a lengthy process that requires the cutting and installation of foundation beams. But once the decking itself is started, the pace seems to accelerate. Almost overnight, there's visible progress.

I'm able to provide considerable assistance to John at this stage of the construction. Admittedly, I make the biggest contributions by bringing work materials and tools to John when he needs them, but what I learn in the process is enlightening for me, particularly when it provides me insight into the structure of my own cabin. Since John built that cabin nearly single-handedly, what I see here at Cabin Number 5 is what lies below the visible surface at my cabin, Number 3. His float cabin construction methods have changed little over the years. John still builds the best cabins on the lake – spoken by a biased source and a highly satisfied customer.

Next on the agenda is design of the lower decks. John has decided to build boat-docking decks on both sides of the cabin, and I'm able to help with the measure-and-construct portion of this construction process. It goes slow, since John never waivers from his endless string of measurements and adjustments to assure that all is precise and correct. During those rare occasions when he makes a mistake, it's not uncommon for the entire job to be disassembled and reconstructed from scratch. What is lost in time is gained in quality and in John's sense that the end product is correct, as he knows it should be. In this regard, John is totally relentless, no matter how much I might try to convince him otherwise. From my somewhat sloppy point of view, I sometimes argue that it's "good enough."

"No one will be able to see it," I often plead.

"But we'll know it's there. So it's not good enough."

With an attitude like that, I lose the argument every time.

✱ ✱ ✱ ✱ ✱

Canada Day – the summer of year two for Number 5. It's a hot day, which reminds me of something Ed says: "Canada has only two seasons – Winter and July First."

John has finished the north side of the lower deck, added since completion of the main upper deck. This area, and a similar section on the south side, will serve as boat docks. Today I'll assist with completion of the dock on the south side.

We begin work at 11 o'clock, which means we'll be working in the heat of the day. But there's always swimming breaks to look forward to.

"Time and a half for me today," I say. "Holiday, you know."

"It's a holiday?"

"Canada Day. You knew that."

"I forgot. That's why the parking was full at the Shinglemill."

"Rocket scientist," I reply. "And aquatic engineer, of course."

The dock construction moves along quickly. I love projects like this, with headway evident almost hour by hour.

We take two swims and break twice for lunch. But by the end of the day, when the sun moves low over the Bunsters, the project is finished, after a satisfying holiday mix of work and play.

# Chapter 13

# Raisin' the Walls

With both the upper and lower decks now complete, the work area is much easier to negotiate – to say nothing of safer. Lumber remnants lie everywhere, but gradually we move the boards and cuttings into neat piles. The floor area is cleared, and the surrounding deck is prepared for the next step – construction of the walls.

John has decided to build the walls horizontally, lying on the deck, with even the plywood exterior installed before we raise them vertically. The process is mostly a one-man operation, so my assistance isn't required. Ed has worked out an elaborate set of computerized blueprints to assist in the design, a major improvement from when John built my cabin twelve years ago.

"Yours was tougher and more time consuming," says John. "Some of the stuff had to be taken apart and redone when I made mistakes. These specs that Dad has developed help a lot."

John works from Ed's drawings as he cuts his window frames, door headers, and intricacies of the structure. On some days, I show up at the work site to assist, but it's mostly a matter of inching boards into position, helping with the starting and stopping of the gas generator for the skill saw, and handing John tools and hardware. For the most part, it's a one-man job.

Over the summer, John slowly puts the walls together. Although a lot is accomplished, from just offshore as I pass by on my way to and from my cabin, little change is noticeable. All of the results rest flat on the deck. Meanwhile, in Hole in the Wall, a neighbor renovates an old float, and a new cabin springs up, including roof. At the south end of the lake, Steve has similarly erected an entire cabin (admittedly modular) over the course of the summer. John feels he's lagging behind these ambitious projects. But his demanding construction standards and attention to budget are the source of the delay, and progress is more significant than meets the passing eye.

Three of the walls include exterior plywood now, while the fourth wall remains uncovered. Two of the plywood walls include the two-foot vertical extension for the roof overhang that will provide a taller loft, and these structures are heavy. One day I ask John how we'll raise the walls.

"Mostly just heave on them, but too much for you and me alone," he says. "I'll get Rick and Dad to help when the time comes. We still might need the turfer."

I walk over to one of the tall walls, grab an end, and try to lift it. When something doesn't budge, it's tough to judge how much more force will be needed to lift it. In this case, I'm convinced the manpower requirements will be considerable, but it's not clear how much will be enough.

"Make sure you call me when you're ready to raise the walls," I say. "It'll be a memorable event, and I don't want to miss it."

"Gettin' close," replies John. "Got some final touches first."

John's final touches can take a while. He's not always fast, but he's invariably thorough.

* * * * *

"**I** could use your help tomorrow," says John when he phones me at my cabin on Thursday night.

"This is it! You're raising the walls!"

"Yup. If I can find some more help. Rick is out of town, but Dad's available. How about you?"

What a sinking feeling. There's almost nothing I wouldn't do to be there, but I've already committed to a business appointment in town.

"Man, I don't know how to be there tomorrow," I whine. "I'm supposed to attend a Chamber of Commerce luncheon meeting, and I hate to cancel. Could we do it early in the morning, or maybe after my meeting – about 2:00?"

"Maybe," says John. But I can tell he's disappointed. "I know it's short notice, but I'd like to get it done before the weekend. Got to go riding on Saturday, you know."

Priorities, of course.

"What about 2:00? I could get to the Shinglemill by 1:00, right after the meeting. Margy would like to be there, too. A little womanpower added to our manpower would help. Plus, I know she'd like to get some photos of the event."

"Okay. I've got some preparation to finish first, so Dad and I might be able to work on that while we're waiting for you."

John doesn't wait for anyone. If it's possible to get the job done before I arrive, he'll try it. Yet, I can't imagine two people raising those walls by themselves. I plan to rush back up the lake as quickly as possible after my morning trip to town.

* * * * *

**B**efore leaving my cabin the next morning, I call John's house at 9:30, looking for an update and another chance to convince John to wait for me before raising the walls.

"John and Ed already left for the lake," says Helen. "They were up early, and John was anxious to get started."

"I'm not surprised. I just hope they wait for me."

"Ed said something about needing to build a support for the winch first. He thinks they'll need the turfer to get the walls up, even with all of you pulling on them."

Ed's engineering mind will provide a realistic slant on the project, as well as a pad of safety. John listens to his dad – most of the time. Still, I hate to miss the morning action. So I suggest to Margy that we start down the lake to town a little early. We can stop at the new cabin and check on the preparations.

At 11:00, I pull the Campion against the outside of the boom at Number 5 and turn off the engine. The first wall is propped slightly upward, barely off the deck and held in position by a pile of blocks. Ed is working on a tall wooden structure that feeds cable to the turfer winch. They're preparing to hoist the first wall, and have already inched it free of the deck with the turfer.

"We stopped to see if we could help for about a half-hour before we need to be in town," I yell across the breakwater boom. "Is there anything we can do."

"No," John yells back. "Still working on the winch. Come on back when your meeting is over."

As I restart the engine and ease away from the boom, I say to Margy: "He won't wait for us, you know. So let's get back up here as soon as possible."

John doesn't wait for anyone.

*  *  *  *  *

After my meeting, we hustle up the lake. While Margy drives, I slip out of my long pants into shorts. The early-September temperature is already climbing, and it will be hot at Number 5.

When we round the point, and turn towards Number 5, we're greeted with a sight that thrills us both. The cabin has a wall!

It may be only the first wall, and there are gaps where the windows and door will be, but it's an honest-to-goodness wall. Finally the cabin has some vertical structure – a major change after months of seemingly nothing. By the end of the day, it will look like a real (almost) cabin.

The smaller and older faded-red Tool Box floats next to the big float with one brownish-orange vertical cabin wall. As we reduce power approaching the breakwater, I notice that the opposite wall is

already angled upward. John and Ed are slowly winching the second wall into position.

Once aboard the float, I'm able to assist a little by sliding the weather-molding at the base of the wall frame into place. But, in general, its mostly John and Ed doing all of the work, handling the turfer, and adjusting the safety rope which will prevent the second wall from tipping beyond vertical once it is fully raised.

Working on the molding, I have plenty of time to absorb the amazing structure of the winch scaffold they have constructed this morning.

With the second wall finally vertical, John braces it in place, and we prepare to raise the third wall without the winch. It's considerably lighter than the first two walls, since it's not yet covered by plywood, plus it's two feet shorter. With the four of us (and Bro supervising), we easily tilt the third wall into position, and John anchors it with braces.

Just as we are thinking about our plan of attack on the last wall (similarly shorter, but with the extra weight of plywood), Bob arrives in his welded-aluminum boat. He's headed up the lake to his cabin and has seen the new structure – the first of many people over the next

few weeks to pull in and take a closer look at the sudden change in the shoreline structure.

"Just in time!" yells John. "You can help us with the next wall."

It's a serendipitous arrival, since the addition of Bob to our crew allows us to raise the last wall without any major problems. It slides into position perfectly, and John tacks on two more braces. Now with all four walls in place and tied together with a lot of braces and a few nails, the structure is ready for winds that will surely come over the next few weeks. Summer is quickly fading into the storms of autumn. And Number 5 is starting to look like a real cabin.

◊ ◊ ◊ ◊ ◊ ◊ ◊

# Chapter 14

# Second Floor

The design for this cabin doesn't really include a second floor, but there's lots of upper structure that's now required. The loft must be built, and the front of the edifice requires construction.

We're now into our second year of construction. I compare the progress during each trip up and down the lake. The cabin is going vertical, a wonderful sign of progress.

Ed is even more involved now, helping John design the peak structure, including the roof cap beam and a center post providing support for the loft. These are huge pieces of timber that will assure extreme strength for the upper portions of the structure.

To be included in this event – raising the roof beam cap – is a special treat for me. I witness a balancing act of ropes and levers, rather than a demonstration of brute force. Together with John and Ed, I help slide the roof beam into position, and then hold it in place while John installs the initial screws.

It's mostly build-as-you-go, although Ed's numerous hours in front of the computer with scaled drawings help keep the dimensions in line. A quarter-inch is too big of an inaccuracy for either Ed or John, so we end up doing some of the work a second or even a third time to

match the plans. In other instances, it's merely an act of strapping on another board here or there as John decides a better way to improve the strength of the upper structure. Call it design flexibility.

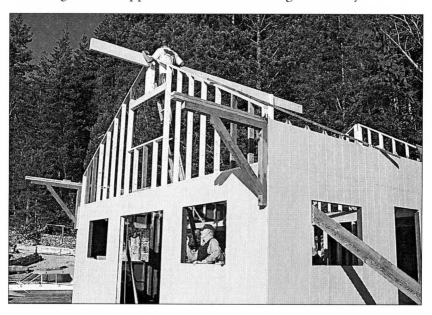

The roof rafters and collar ties (strapping boards) go up, precisely measured and aligned. Rick is helping out a lot now, with both brothers spending hours-on-end on the roof, day after day, finishing the rafters. Margy and I are mostly interested observers at this point, since Rick and John form a formidable team that an added person could only interrupt in function. When they work together, it's often with a form of nonverbal communication based on knowledge of wood skills and years of functioning as a team.

In fact, many of my self-assigned tasks at this time are minor, but seemingly helpful to John. I hold the base of ladders during his high ventures and hand him tools and food. My proclaimed duties may be minimal, but I know they're appreciated. If nothing else, I'm there to help with the cleanup and to support the master on the job.

Much of the work consists of one-man tasks that enhance quality in the finished cabin. Drip strips are installed between the upper and lower walls to assure wood joints stay dry. Trim on the eves of the roof promotes proper drainage. Paint that will be later covered by another layer of wood assures a rot-free product.

John is now fully two years into the project, and he's racing towards the point where all exterior openings will be closed. The roof, doors, windows, and the chimney area form major gaps that will need to be filled. It's a race against the coming rains of winter.

# Chapter 15

# The Church

Although geographically immense, this lake is a small community. Accidents in this unforgiving environment can be disastrous. Even the indirect effects of an incident that happens here can be significant. And so it was at this point in the cabin construction process.

Comparable to a pilot hearing about an airplane crash (involving a friend, a favourite airport, or the same model of aircraft), a tragic incident on the lake in early autumn becomes an eye-opener. A dedicated pilot doesn't quit flying, and a determined float cabin owner doesn't give up his lifestyle. But this incident certainly gets our attention.

Peter's cabin is one of the most luxurious on the lake, originally designed as a bed-and-breakfast that never got off the ground. From the moment Margy and I saw the cabin, just off to the right of our normal route to Hole in the Wall, we called it "the Church." Grandiose by Powell Lake standards, the two-story structure boasted a wall of windows facing the North Sea, not unlike the stained glass structure common to churches.

The idea for this cabin was a good one, but like other remote real estate, the concept failed to consider the most important water-estate criteria – location, location, location. In fact, other places on

Powell Lake not accessible by road have suffered a similar fate in recent decades. A lodge near Olsen's Landing now sits idle, with the for-sale price dwindling month-after-month. Prior entrepreneurs attempted to promote this lodge as a get-away destination. Even with a dedicated boat, the *Mugwump*, standing by to serve potential tourists, the lodge and its cute cabins failed to find financial prosperity. Getting there isn't just part of the problem, it is the problem.

When Peter purchases the cabin, it isn't as a bed-and-breakfast, but he does plan to entertain clients as part of his business. As a Canadian, Peter now lives in California, with his new float cabin serving as a summer retreat. I first meet Peter when he purchases a copy of *Up the Lake* from me at a book-signing event in town, and I subsequently introduce him to John. Peter needs help in maintaining his cabin, and John readily comes to his aid.

Margy and I keep in touch with Peter during the off-season, checking his float when we go up and down the lake. Although his location at the northeast tip of Henderson Bay is a bit off our normal track, we see it from the distance on every trip. But we occasionally

swing close and snap a photo to email to Peter. He's a summer-only resident here, and we're trying to entice him to visit in the winter season.

This summer, Peter and his friend, Wayne, spend a summer enjoying the lake, entertaining Margy and me (the other Wayne) at their luxurious floating cabin. "Luxurious," when applied to float cabins includes a spiral staircase to the second floor and a full-fledged connoisseur's kitchen, which are novelties on the lake. Such an environment is appropriate for a gourmet cook like Peter.

When Peter and Wayne depart for California in September, they visit John and me at Number 5 on their way down the lake. In the bow of their 17-foot Boston Whaler is an ice chest full of food they have removed from their cabin refrigerator. Rather than throw it away, they offer it to us.

"I can't take much," I tell Peter. "My fridge at the cabin is pretty tiny and awfully full. But maybe John can take most of it home with him."

"Sure," pipes John. "I'll take it."

I try to imagine John eating caviar and artichoke hearts. Maybe Jimmy or Terry will get a gift from him. In any case, the food won't go to waste.

Peter and Wayne then hustle down the lake in mid-afternoon, intent on making it as far as Vancouver today, not an easy goal, considering the two ferries they'll need to catch.

\* \* \* \* \*

Three weeks later, I motor down the lake in the morning, planning to meet John at Number 5. I'm not sure what project is on the schedule today, but he hasn't missed a workday at the new cabin all week. Work on the upper portion of the front wall is probably on tap.

When I cross the North Sea, I'm obliviously intent on Cassiar Island ahead, not even glancing at the Church. As I pull up to Number 5 in the Campion, I can see that I won't be needed today. John and Rick are already standing near the top of two parallel ladders, working under the front eave. I stop long enough to say hello, and ask if there is anything I can do to help.

"Not really," admits John. "You can just hang around, if you want to."

Not exactly my kind of excitement. When John and Rick are working together, anyone that steps into their world can do nothing but interfere. At least I'm wise enough to recognize this. So I leave, headed back to my cabin, and that's not a bad thing – any excuse for a morning boat ride on a calm lake is fine by me.

On my second crossing of the North Sea today, I apparently don't glance at Peter's cabin. Because if I did, I would have undoubtedly recognized that it's no longer there.

In just a few minutes, I'm pulling into Hole in the Wall, while Margy is motoring out in our tin boat. It seems a little unusual, but I'm not particularly surprised. Maybe she's just going for a morning boat ride, like me.

"Helen just called!" yells Margy, as I drift up next to her. "Peter's cabin burned down."

"What!" I can hardly believe what I'm hearing. "Are you sure?"

"It's pretty confusing. Peter called from Palm Springs, trying to reach John. The RCMP phoned Peter to explain that his cabin burned down last night. A crew boat heading up the lake this morning saw smoke, and went over to investigate. Supposedly, it burned right to the waterline. So he's trying to reach John, to make sure it's really his cabin."

There can be a lot of jumbled information about things like this. Cabins move around on this lake. Sometimes a cabin is found floating free, and nobody can figure out who it belongs to. The location of specific cabins on the lake isn't well documented. If a cabin burned down, maybe it wasn't Peter's, after all.

"Take the tin boat back, and I'll pick you up," I say.

In just a few minutes, we're blasting down the lake at nearly full power, angling to the left after First Narrows, headed directly towards Peter's cabin, or whatever remains of it. We're hoping for the best, but fearing the worst.

I don't see the cabin at the tip of the bay, but we still have quite a ways to go. Then I see smoke, a gray smoldering plume, with no obvious structure beneath it. Peter's cabin is gone.

When we pull up against the boom, only the float remains, and it's severely burned. The few shapes sticking up from the waterline are low piles of destroyed metal, intensely warped and still smoldering.

There's nothing we can do here. It's certainly not wise to go onto the float in this still-burning condition. There's evidence here that will be needed when the authorities investigate, and we don't want to taint possible signs of the source of the fire. Nor do we want to be accused of tampering with evidence.

"Let's get John," I state.

After all, Peter phoned John, asking his verification of the burning. And we can be at Number 5 in just a few minutes.

\* \* \* \* \*

**W**hen I pull up outside John's boom, the two brothers are still on their ladders, Rick holding a two-by-four, while John nails it into place. John looks over at me, his brow arched in an obvious question: *Now what?*

I yell across the breakwater: "Peter's cabin is gone. Burned down completely, still smoking."

"No way!"

"I'm serious. Your mom called Margy, trying to get hold of you. Peter phoned from California. He says the RCMP called him this morning."

"Well we can't leave right now," says John.

An odd statement, considering the circumstances. In fact, I almost have to pry John and Rick away from their work, as if a burned cabin is a routine thing. In a way, John is right. What's to be gained by interrupting work for a cabin that no longer exists. But there's a note of disbelief in John's attitude. After all, I've led him on many wild goose chases before.

"Are you sure it burned down?" he questions.

"Look, John, we just came by the cabin. Or what used to be a cabin. It's gone."

"You're sure."

"Absolutely. Now let's get going!"

Finally, Rick and John climb down from their ladders, reluctantly

secure their tools, and head for John's boat. Margy and I are already back at the smoking float, when John and Rick pull up in the Hourston.

"Holy crap!" yells John. "It really did burn down."

We hover near Peter's breakwater, agreeing that we shouldn't go aboard the float or even onto the nearby shore to get a closer look. The on-shore shed seems to have survived without burn marks, and the pole-mounted wind generator sits untouched. The only other remaining structure that seems to have come through unscathed is the breakwater and a small extension of dock at what used-to-be the front deck.

"Man, I just finished building that front dock," says John. "And all my other work is down the tubes. Even the stove and refrigerator, and the spiral staircase, are completely melted."

"I'm going to call Peter," I yell across to John from the Campion. "Anything you want me to tell him, besides the obvious."

"He'll want to know if the float is salvageable," replies John. "Tell him I think it's damaged beyond repair, but I won't know for sure until I can go aboard."

I pull out my cell phone and make one of the most difficult telephone calls I've ever had to make.

* * * * *

The cause of the fire is never determined. On this lake, not a lot of attention is paid to the formal investigative requirements paid homage to in the nearby town. At Peter's request, John brings the RCMP to the site a few days later in his Hourston. The constable hops onto shore to get a closer look, but refuses to step onto the float in the interest of personal safety. Even after several days, the wreckage was still smoldering, and the police are more intent on determining whether there might be a body in the charred remains. When, from their on-shore vantage point, the constable becomes comfortable with the lack of a body, the case is virtually closed.

An insurance investigator similarly is transported to the site a few days after this, and he sifts through some of the wreckage. There's not much to inspect, but the severity of the fire is verified when a charred 100-pound propane tank is found onshore, propelled there by the intensity of the blaze.

We're all concerned about arson, although there's no direct evidence. Certainly, Peter secured his cabin well before departing for California three weeks prior to the blaze. He remembers not only turning off the propane tanks, a normal precaution during extended periods of absence, he even recalls disconnecting the valve fittings and installing the protective plastic caps. That's a lot more than any of us do when turning off the propane, but it's typical of Peter.

Yet, there had to be a source of ignition. Could it have been a transient squatter who decided to move into the cabin? Maybe what happened was an accident during such an occurrence, which is a more pleasant prospect than pure arson. Still, it's not a comfortable feeling. Even John begins to talk about fire insurance, while his cabin is still under construction. But before the tragedy fades in our minds, another false alarm arises on a cold and windy Saturday night, less than a week after the fire.

Margy answers the phone at our cabin, finding an excited Peter on the other end of the line.

"I just got a call from a friend in Powell River who was listening to his police scanner. Another cabin just burned down, near the Clover Lake logging dock. Can you go up there and see what happened?"

We would do almost anything for Peter, except this. It's already dark, and that coupled with the wind on the lake makes such a request futile.

"We can't go tonight," replies Margy, without hesitation. "But we'll go up there first thing in the morning, and call you right away."

The next morning, we cruise up to the logging dark under nearly-calm conditions. At first we see no evidence of a fire. Then, inspecting along the shore north of the dock, we encounter a charred float, with only a little rubble aboard. The float itself has survived to see another day. In fact, a little charring of the logs can provide anti-rot protection. There has been a recent fire here, that's for sure, but it looks like the float was nearly empty when the blaze occurred. Strangely, tied to the burnt float is another full-size float, riding in formation and completely unharmed.

When we return to Hole in the Wall, we report what we've found to Peter, promising to update him when we learn more, which doesn't take long.

John has already heard about the fire: "Mike saw it when he was riding his quad yesterday on Dalgliesh Main. I hear it was an old shack that some guy burned down on purpose, to clear the float for a new cabin. Happens all the time."

It may happen all the time, but this guy sure picked a bad week to set his cabin on fire.

* * * * *

Our anxiety regarding the fire fades with time. Still, both John and I remain concerned over the danger of arson on the lake. In town, a trailer truck mysteriously goes up in flames near the barge depot. And everyone on the lake continues to talk about Peter's cabin, and what may have caused the fire.

What's needed is closure, and part of that comes when Peter hires John to haul away the destroyed float, in preparation for the sale of his site. Unfortunately, Peter has decided that he'll not be returning to Powell Lake. His memories of the tragedy are too strong. But the spot will be a good site for a new cabin, once the old float is removed.

John tows the badly burned float down to Number 5, where it sits next to his new cabin. On a dreary March afternoon, only two days after the official arrival of spring, we sift through the charred remains, loading fused metal pieces onto a raft to tow down the lake and discard at the recycling center. When we sift through the wreckage, we find nothing of value left to report to Peter.

It's a sad day of work, and a dirty soot-covered one, too. But this is the beginning of spring, a period when new beginnings are easy to visualize. Even here in this burned mass, we ponder an ending to this ordeal. From the ashes of life come new beginnings.

# Chapter 16

# Green Roof

"My last two roofs have been blue," says John. "What do you think about green?"

When John asks a question like this, I'm not sure he really needs my advice. In this case, it seems he has already made up his mind.

"Green would look nice," I reply. "Especially that rich green on the roof of some of the cabins on the lake."

Green it is. But it takes a while for the roofing material to arrive at the local lumber yard. You can order anything in town, but getting it can take some time. Most big items come by barge from Vancouver or on a truck that must navigate two ferries. The exception is the occasional item that's available on Vancouver Island. Even that requires a ferry.

So we wait for the green roof sheets to arrive.

After several weeks, we finally have the metal. But getting it to the cabin is a slightly different drill. John arranges to have the sheets delivered to the Shinglemill. Meanwhile, I bring the raft down from Number 5, towed behind the Campion. The big delivery truck shows up with exactly what we need – a crane!

With the raft positioned at the Shinglemill launch ramp, the truck drives close enough to load the sheets directly onto the raft. John, Rick, and Bro supervise.

I start northbound, towing the raft, while John drives his boat, with Rick and Bro aboard, to meet me at Number 5. Then we off-load the sheets, and stack them on the deck. Finally the process is complete, and the roof is ready to be installed. The crane has been quite an extravagance for us.

"I vote for hiring a crane whenever we need to move anything," I suggest.

"Good luck," says John.

But he too has appreciated the luxury. Too bad we can't afford it every time.

Rick and John do most of the roofing, while I hold ladders and cut sheets of tarpaper that serve as waterproofing under the metal roof. The first few sheets take an entire day, as John tries to determine the precise alignment at the front of the cabin that will result in a vertically-aligned position of the sheets at the rear.

I depart Number 5 late in the afternoon, while John and Rick are still working on the second narrow sheet. When I cruise past the cabin the next day, the sheets are gone – John has decided the installation of the first two sheets wasn't properly aligned, so he'll start all over again.

Two days later, John and Rick begin again, this time making substantial progress by early afternoon. I'm there again to assist, but my primary job is to stay out of the way. And to stay warm and dry, which isn't easy, considering the circumstances. It's now late October, and today is a typically cool and showery day. But a little rain won't stop these roofers.

We make it through the first few sheets, and this time John is satisfied with the alignment. I hand up sheets to Rick, who pushes them farther towards the peak, where John slides them into position. Then Rick, working with a tape measure, makes the final alignment relative to a leveling string that runs the entire length of the cabin.

Days are getting shorter now, but Rick and John are determined to get the first side of the roof finished today, and it looks like they might succeed. But several times we have to stop when the rain pounds down hard. Light rain showers aren't going to stop them, but it sure looks cold up there.

Between downpours, the conditions are good, though a bit too cold for my taste. Since I'm not doing much work, mostly waiting for the next sheet to be hoisted, it's probably colder from my perspective.

The rain gets more intense, and I take refuge under the partially completed roof. I can hear the heavy precipitation striking the metal, knowing that John and Rick are up there getting doused. But then the weather clears temporarily, followed almost immediately by another shower, and the hearty roofers continue, roofin' in the rain. By sunset the south side is nearly finished.

# Chapter 17

# Lockup

John doesn't make his goal of lockup prior to winter moving in. We didn't make it in time for the rainy season, though that's primarily a matter of choice. John is still waiting for an acceptable bargain on a sliding glass door, and the chimney is similarly delayed. If you wait long enough in this town, everything eventually goes on sale. Meanwhile, the roof is complete, all of the walls are solid, and the windows are in place. The cabin is secure and safe for the rainy season, when everything involved in the construction process goes into slow motion. Lockup will be a significant milestone, being able to shut the door at the end of a day of work, and seal off the interior. After two and a half years, we're finally on the verge of meeting this goal.

John has the wood stove, a second-hand structure that's in good shape, needing only a few repairs. I help him lift it into place, elevated on a metal riser he has built, and John talks about how he'll sit on the sofa (not yet purchased) and watch the fire through the stove's glass door.

"The sofa will be over here, and the stovepipe will clear that beam by the amount required to get proper fire insurance," he says. "We'll be able to sit and look outside, watching the stove at the same time."

"Good location," I say. "We'll be able to kick back and watch all of the boats going by."

"I can build a shelf there," he says, pointing to the space below the big second-floor window. "Put some treasures there, like the shelf I built for Margy at Number 3."

Yes, Cabin Number 3 has set a wonderful standard. And now John gets to improve on his dream over that masterpiece of construction. It's hard to imagine that life could get any better than this.

But there's an awful lot still to be done. Where will all of the interior appliances come from? What about counters and furniture? Yet, these are moot points when a cabin is this close to lockup.

\* \* \* \* \*

As summer approaches (and still no sliding door or chimney), the final layer of plywood for the floor is next. I help John with cutting and positioning the pieces and screwing them down. It's a time-consuming task that John tackles mostly by himself over the next few days.

Chimney acquisition is a delayed, while John closely compares structural considerations and price, but it's finally time to proceed. He orders what's needed for piping, but ducts of the right length aren't in stock. So again we wait.

Meanwhile, the top portion of the chimney and the cap are available, so we work on that installation. John climbs into position on the roof, while I hoist the stovepipe up to him.

The lower portion of the stovepipe, inside the cabin, will be installed last. In the meantime, the above-roof portion will provide a weather-tight seal once the flashing is complete. One step closer to lockup.

The only remaining link in the process is the sliding glass door. John has been holding off, looking for a used door. But finding one in acceptable condition isn't easy. Finally, he locates a reasonably-priced new door in Sechelt, and it's worth the ferry trip from Saltery Bay. With the door finally in place, it official – lockup!

John proudly strolls over to the sliding glass door, locks it, and then checks all the windows. He takes a quick look around to assure everything is in its place. Then he steps out the side door, locking it behind him for the first time.

◊ ◊ ◊ ◊ ◊ ◊

# Epilogue

# The Long Ride

Lockup is a momentous occasion, but John is still a long way from finished. The interior will still require a lot of time and attention to detail. The inside of the cabin is now bare. Before this becomes a home, many interior construction chores lie ahead. There's a long list of furnishings that need to be found or purchased. The tradeoff between waiting for bargains to appear and simply going out and buying necessary items equates back to time and the bottom line – money. Nothing can slow a project more than funding, and John's situation is no exception.

The hunt is on for a propane refrigerator and stove, manual water pump, sink, furniture, and propane bottles and fittings. One-by-one, John adds them to his inventory. There are shelves and cabinets to build, insulation to install – a seemingly endless list.

Bit by bit, the inside takes shape, and even the exterior continues to develop. A porch on both sides has long been part of the plan, but these extensions have waited until all settles down. Now John tackles that project with all the determination that he puts into every venture. But this addition is a more leisurely process, now that the cabin has reached lockup. It gradually changes the look of the cabin, making the structure more complete, and more like a home.

The journey has been spectacular. Yes, there have been problems, compromises, and plenty of delays waiting for weather and materials. But John now has his cabin, and it's a fine structure.

It's been a long voyage. But he did it his way. And I was privileged to be along for the ride.

# About the Author

From 1980 to 2005, Wayne Lutz was Chairman of the Aeronautics Department at Mount San Antonio College in Los Angeles. He also served 20 years as a U.S. Air Force C-130 aircraft maintenance officer. His educational background includes a B.S. degree in physics from the University of Buffalo and an M.S. in systems management from the University of Southern California. The author is a flight instructor with 7000 hours of flying experience.

For the past three decades, he has spent summers in Canada, exploring remote regions in his Piper Arrow, camping next to his airplane. The author resides in a floating cabin on Canada's Powell Lake in all seasons, and occasionally in a city-folk condo in Bellingham, Washington. His writing genres include regional Canadian publications and science fiction.

In the rain – John (left) with Bro and the author

**Cabin Number 5** is the 9th in a series of volumes focusing on the unique places and memorable people of coastal British Columbia

## Order at:
www.PowellRiverBooks.com

## Coastal BC Living Blog
PowellRiverBooks.blogspot.com